NAME IT AND CLAIM IT?

NAME IT
and CLAIM IT?

Prosperity Preaching in the Black Church

STEPHANIE Y. MITCHEM

THE PILGRIM PRESS
CLEVELAND

The Pilgrim Press, 700 Prospect Avenue, East, Cleveland, Ohio 44115-1100
thepilgrimpress.com
© 2007 Stephanie Y. Mitchem

Scripture quotations, unless otherwise noted, are from the New Revised Standard Version of the Bible, © 1989 by the Division of Christian Education of the National Council of Churches of Christ in the United States of America and are used by permission. Changes have been made for inclusivity.

12   11   10   09   08   07   5   4   3   2   1

Library of Congress Cataloging-in-Publication Data

Mitchem, Stephanie Y., 1950–
    Name it and claim it? : prosperity preaching in the Black church /
Stephanie Y. Mitchem.
        p. cm.
    ISBN 978-0-8298-1709-6 (alk. paper)
    1. African Americans—Religion.   2. Wealth—Religious aspects—
Christianity.   3. Preaching.   I. Title.

BR563.N4M595 2007
277.3'08208996073—dc22   2007008546

Contents

D uring the course of this research, I attended services at several churches throughout the United States, five of which I discuss in this book. Writing this book was an adventure in understanding black religious life today, which I firmly believe would not have made sense without actually visiting the churches and using their own religious educational materials. The churches discussed here are pastored by some of the more well-known prosperity preachers: Creflo Dollar (Atlanta, Georgia), Keith Butler (Detroit, Michigan), Leroy Thompson (Darrow, Louisiana), Johnnie Coleman (Chicago, Illinois), and Rev. Ike (New York City). These five fall into two of the three church categories that I identify as focused on prosperity. This book is very different because of these visits. What I would have written without these experiences and conversations would have presented a skewed view.

It is important to remember that the three categories I outline and the few churches discussed provide but a limited sample of prosperity preaching in black communities. They are presented, however, to afford a greater understanding of this religious phenomenon in black communities as it has developed in the past and is lived today. With understanding, I hope that we African Americans are careful and deliberate in shaping our religious futures.

I want to make it clear that I deliberately did not attempt to interview the leadership of these church communities. Writing this book has been an exercise of understanding what is happening when black folks think about "naming it and claiming it," rather than how their leaders happen to frame it.

Finally, analysis of African American religions, especially tracing one facet from the past to the present, is a process of stepping into the streams of a people's faith lives. These in themselves are sacred. I acknowledge black people across the African Diaspora who have struggled and believed. I am in awe of the expressions of love and hope, firmly grounded in faith, that surface in strange places. Or, as my old auntie used to say, "Even lilies can grow on dung heaps."

I especially thank my editor at The Pilgrim Press, Kim Martin Sadler, who has encouraged and supported this work and whose phone conversations helped me to find the words to talk about our spirituality of longing.

INTRODUCTION

African Americans are religiously complicated people, with a rich and creative history. Religion and culture are so intertwined in black communities as to be indistinguishable from each other. The happenings of religious life are of importance to us, becoming the focus of music, artwork, and family arguments, as well as community life. When religious news happens it becomes a topic of conversation in black barbershops, beauty shops, and senior centers. Prosperity churches and preachers have been a hot topic among African Americans. Defining themselves as Christian, prosperity churches have theologies that stress that God's favor is shown to believers in an immediate, material way. Money and material benefits are blessings granted the believer in this thinking and, furthermore, are guaranteed by God's promise. These are distinctive Christian theologies that bring some new things to discussions.

Throughout black communities, the antics of preachers along with prosperity ideas from the churches make their way into everyday conversation. For instance, the query "How are you?" might elicit the response "I'm blessed" from black adults. The phrase itself is rooted in prosperity thought. Or it is not unusual to hear of someone headed for a Sunday service at a traditional black church, but keeping the television on one or another prosperity preacher while getting dressed. Of course, prosperity ideas and churches are not exclusive to black communities. But the impact may be felt more deeply than in white American communities: a few million members of prosperity churches from among white Americans with a greater religious diversity (including Jewish, Mormon, Mennonite, as well as traditional Christian communities) are proportionately not as significant a percentage as a few million members are from black, mostly Christian, communities. Prosperity religions have had a wide impact on African American religious life. But the numbers alone are not enough to answer the question: What are the *meanings* of these prosperity churches for black communities? The question is not as simple as it seems but advocates using a wider lens to understand the multilayered influences of prosperity churches and theologies.

Even at a casual glance, a variety of other questions arise from the prosperity-focused theologies' sociological and theological structures. Do they redefine ministry in black communities? How are gender roles and family woven into the structures of theologies of prosperity? In what ways do television and Internet usage by prosperity churches change the shape of black religious community? Why do some churches with theologies of prosperity so often align themselves with conservative political groups? Who is God in these theologies?

This book takes a closer look at African American prosperity churches and their theologies. I use a wide lens to consider prosperity theologies and churches in the context of the African American community and the black church, rather than as isolated and incidental phenomena. I also track some of the sociological and theological changes in black life that are attributable to theologies of prosperity. In the context of black community and religious life, I focus on three main prosperity church groupings (which could be considered denominational). I also analyze the contemporary dynamics of African American theologies of prosperity, which are historically grounded but have new ideas that developed in the late twentieth century.

While theologies and churches are the center of this book, the larger themes of sociological and spiritual contexts became clearer to me as I sat through many services. While visiting prosperity churches I was struck by the fervor of their members and wondered why black people are so strongly drawn to these churches. Clearly, there are issues resolved for the person who converts to prosperity churches, and I wanted to absorb these religious understandings that yet remain in the context of black American life.

In the process of thinking about prosperity preaching in the broadest possible terms, I bring in as many aspects as possible, including historical views. In one chapter, I also include stories about the impact of prosperity preaching on black life. One of the stories is from Delores, a black woman whose pastor attempted to use prosperity preaching to grow the congregation; in her experience, his efforts failed miserably. Another story focuses on an unpleasant public encounter between a black seminary and a local prosperity-style preacher. Throughout the book, I included many voices of writers and thinkers in religion and other fields whose ideas have relevance to this discussion. The point I am stressing is simply this: prosperity preaching does not just impact those churches' members but has become an issue of import, which has other implications about national life to many African Americans. Prosperity preaching is a sign of the times.

To explore all these ideas, this book has three general sections. The first section, chapters 1 through 3, explores the shape of black communities and those things that make prosperity churches attractive to black members. Chapter 1 begins with the black church, which has played a significant role in the lives of African Americans. While this is a fact that no one can deny, has the social and spiritual dominance of the black church actually abetted the rise of prosperity churches? Do the culturally learned action and response patterns of black church members set them up for unquestioned acceptance of prosperity preachers? Do other aspects of the black church, such as status and social class structures, make prosperity churches attractive options?

These sociological factors alone do not explain why black people are attracted to prosperity churches. Chapter 2 examines ways that poverty and oppression have shaped African American spirituality. Poverty is a reality and wealth could not be accumulated in black communities. Long-term legal segregation and the effects of institutionalized racism become integral to African American spiritual life. A spirituality of longing is a term that best describes the result of these combined realities.

A general description of theologies of prosperity and how they use or address aspects of black religious life are the focus of chapter 3. The two stories, one of Delores and the other involving a black seminary, are windows through which to view prosperity preaching. This leads into the second section of the book—chapters 4 through 6. This section describes three general types of prosperity churches.

There are some prosperity churches that were developed from within the black community. Chapter 4 looks at as examples of these, the ministries of Daddy Grace and Father Divine. However, two alternate ways of addressing prosperity from within the black community via religion are considered. The next type of prosperity church flows from white ministers Kenneth Hagin and Kenneth Copeland. Examples of black ministers from the Hagin/Copeland school are discussed in chapter 5: Creflo Dollar, Leroy Thompson, and Fred Price. The third type of prosperity church follows the metaphysical Science of Mind and Unity thought. Barbara King, Rev. Ike, and Johnnie Colemon have built thriving ministries using these ideas, which are discussed in chapter 6.

The last section of the book, chapters 7 and 8, considers the impact of these churches and their theologies on black communities and the black church. Chapter 7 looks at theologies of prosperity in black communities as part of larger trends that are reshaping black identities. The drive toward greater consumerism and the ongoing desire to be fully accepted into the United States as a people leads to new dynamics in black communal life that are expressed in religious language. Finally, chapter 8 analyzes the wider impact of prosperity churches' theological constructions for the black church. This is explored through the question: What is the "good news" of theologies of prosperity and does it really align with the gospel? The other side of prosperity theologies is their related meaning for black communities' theological and religious development. Theologies of prosperity are changing the shape of black religious life, and I discuss these challenges.

By deliberately keeping the focus of this book wide, by historically and sociologically grounding my arguments, I have two objectives. The first, the easiest to state, is to paint a portrait of black religious life as it is developing, as we continue into the twenty-first century. The changes we are experiencing are often hard to see because they are so close to us. But these new churches and ways of preaching highlight the scope of the changes with both frightening aspects and important lessons to be learned across black communities.

My second objective is related to the first. I hope to encourage deeper discussions of the directions and meaning of black religious life in many places in black communities. I hope others will trace much different lines of argument than mine, uncover new facts, and create dialogues that are about African American religiosity and extend into analyses of the future of black culture.

AT THE DOORS OF THE BLACK CHURCH

My elderly aunt, with her husband, has been very involved in the African Methodist Episcopal (AME) church's lay leaders movement. Together, they visited just about every state and attended most AME conventions. When my aunt came to visit me this past year, we attended a local AME church. We attended the service on Founders' Day, so there were extra speeches, an exceptional choir performance, and a former pastor preaching. In the middle of all the joyful activity, my aunt leaned over and whispered: "You know, the AME church is losing membership." "Why?" I whispered back. Her reply: "It's the megachurches, the megachurches."

Any discussion about prosperity churches in black communities (especially to find answers to the "whys") must include the wider story of the black church in America—not just as it is at this moment, but also as the church developed. A whispered conversation with my aunt brought this home for me in several ways.

With my aunt, I attended a historic celebration of a congregation of the AME church that had been in the neighborhood community for more than a hundred years. This aunt had lived through legal segregation, a move from the South to the North, and the civil rights and black power movements, always grounded by her religious faith. She witnessed significant changes in the possibilities for the success of her family but she is now witnessing changes in the very structures of the religious life that gave her strength. She sounded a warning about the future of the black church. She identified megachurches as the culprits, but there is no single place to lay blame. The problems that helped give rise to the megachurches are connected to the growth and social acceptance of prosperity churches. The stories of both need to be told and their meanings for black communities explored. Prosperity churches, however, must be understood in a wider framework, especially the context that gave rise to and that supports this thinking in black communities.

My aunt's perspectives give clues about how the structures of black churches have influenced African American communities. To further discuss prosperity churches, in particular in African American communities, we begin by looking at the black church itself, some of its meanings, part of the history, and important contemporary changes.

ABOUT THE BLACK CHURCH

I had an uncle who would not go into a church. Although I never heard the full story, I knew that he had become angry at all churches and refused to attend any. His wife, however, regularly attended church. Because she did not drive, he would, without fail, take her to church and sit in the car with coffee and a newspaper and cigarettes every week. The church members, like our family, all knew what was happening and why. I would contend that the church members would understand that my uncle "belonged" to them, whether he entered the church building or not. Notwithstanding his anger with all churches, I know that he had a belief in God and supported his wife's participation. This is one way to understand what the black church has meant in the black community—it is beyond membership or even a particular belief. Instead, it can be described as sets of relationships—between people and with the Divine. Those relationships still define the life and experiences of the majority of black people in their communities.

The black church is neither a single institution nor a formal organization of all the churches to which African Americans belong. Ethicist Barbara Holmes describes the black church in this way:

> The black church has an actual and a meta-actual form. It inhabits the imagination of its people in ways that far exceed its reach. Although it is no longer a truly invisible institution, it will always be invisible to some extent because it embodies a spiritual idea. This idea is grounded not only in history but also in the narratives and myths of an oppressed people. The black church has been a spiritual wellspring . . . one of the few safe spaces in an unsafe world.[1]

Her definition points out the mythic quality of the black church: it is real and not imaginary, because it helps to shape religious and social meanings for African Americans. During enslavement and oppression in this country, the black church became a singular and important way for black people to get in touch with their humanity and goodness, despite the ways white communities enacted political, social, or theological degradation against them. Laying claim to identities that are different from those expressed by the majority culture emphasizes the creativity that black people bring to the life and activity of religion. Holmes' definition points toward ways that churches have been able to provide leadership in black communities. Her definition highlights the sense of *home* that black people experience in their churches.

But black church life is and has been complex. Even with many positive stories to call forth, some other churches have been negative influences in black communities, failing to fulfill ministerial charges on behalf of their members or neighborhoods. Just about every black person can tell a story about someone who has felt mistreated by his or her church. The mistreatment might be an experience from an interaction with the pastoral staff or might be the result of power struggles between members.

Humanities professor and Baptist preacher Michael Eric Dyson contrasts the stated theology with the practice in some churches and sharply demonstrates how some black churches fail.

> Black religious oratory has too often been employed to line the pockets of materialistic ministers or cause vulnerable women to swoon and sexually submit under the hypnotic sway of eloquence. And the genius of black rhetoric has too often been employed to obscure personal and professional misconduct. . . . While black ministers rail against the sexual deviance of rappers, teen mothers, and gays and lesbians, they often fail to confront the rituals of seduction they practice from the pulpit. Bedding women is nearly a sport in some churches.[2]

Adding layers of complexity to any study of the black church are the political and theological dimensions. Politically, African Americans were not granted citizenship in the United States until the end of slavery and the passage of the Fourteenth Amendment to the Constitution in 1868. It was not until the passage of the Twenty-Fourth Amendment to the Constitution in 1964, which barred poll taxes and other barriers against black voting in the South, that there was a sense of full citizenship for all black Americans. While Dyson critiqued abusive aspects of the black church, he also identified what he termed the "radical remnant."[3] This radical remnant connects theology with politics and culture in order to bring about social justice. In this connection, God is seen as an actor in public events. With such thinking the black church could affect the shape of society.

> The black church provided a place for white unions to meet and organize when no else would have them. It helped to establish buying clubs and cooperatives. It agitated to increase wages for workers. It helped to improve federal agricultural policies. . . . And the black church pushed for better schools and black voting rights. In fact, union culture was shot through with black religious sentiment.[4]

But the black church is by no means a monolith. From enslavement through the civil rights and black power movements, the black church had no single voice to address injustices. Some black pastors barred their members from participating in unions; this occurred when black workers were brought from the South to work for the Ford Motor Company. At the same time, some black pastors encouraged participation in the union movement. Some black church communities marched for civil rights; others found such social activism counter to the tenets of Christianity. These political differences of opinion sprang from divergent operative theologies.

What should the role of the church be in the face of oppression? The answers the black churches found were not uniform but were based in the theologies that informed the life of a specific church community or denomination. Since the black church is, as Holmes said, a meta-actual or virtual reality, theologies that are conflicting and contradictory can inform different denominations. For example, on questions of injustice, if a church is informed by a theology that defines its work as *only* dealing with the spiritual, that denomination would determine that ending oppression on this earth would not be part of their ministry. If another denomination was informed by a theology that saw God as the only One who is entitled to seek vengeance and grant mercy, then it might follow that justice would be given in God's time. There have even been some black denominations that have accepted the "curse of Ham" theology developed by white theologians during enslavement, a theology that interpreted blackness itself as a sign of God's disfavor of black-skinned people. This theology also determined that black enslavement was a natural consequence of this curse and, therefore, black people were meant to be slaves to white people by God's decree. Of course, there were other theologies that defined the God-created goodness of all people, and a church was viewed as a place to give succor to those in need. In other words, a denomination would act in accord with its stated theology.

There are different black Christian denominations. The African Methodist Episcopal church is different from Progressive Baptist convention, which is yet different from the experiences of black Episcopalians. This diversity is not a barrier to black faith experiences because a commitment to one church or another is not intended to be a barrier to communication with God in the midst of community. The underlying motif in black communities is that each person should seek a religious home in which to express his or her spiritual dimension. A single family may have diverse religious affiliations among its members. My own family is an example where the different members have belonged to various churches, including AME, Roman Catholic, Episcopal, Seventh Day Adventist, Mennonite, Unitarian, Unity, United Methodist, and the Nation of Islam. In black communities, finding the best way to communicate with God and live one's faith are important values.

Theology and politics, as well as denominational affiliation and a sense of home, are aspects of black church life. These concepts will also surface in some ways in the stories of black prosperity churches. But to understand the present, we need to consider the past, because some portions of the history of the black church influence our realities today.

For the most part, African Americans have historically been involved with various denominations of Christian churches, even as that Christian focus has become less exclusive and more diversified. Churches were the center of black social, political, and, at times, economic life; these churches were the first institutions over which black Americans had some control. Becoming an ordained minister and leading a church has long been considered a worthy career path in black communities. Being the pastor's wife or family offered a level of social and sometimes economic security in the midst of the black community. The commonality of this career path in black communities is the heart of a somewhat humorous folk saying: "Black folks ain't good for nothing but preaching and teaching." Religious and educational careers were seriously important for black communities after the Emancipation Proclamation that ended enslavement. Preachers and teachers aided black communities in myriad ways, such as promoting black literacy campaigns.

The connection of black churches to their communities was not the result of a dogmatic list of God's rules-rewards-punishment. Instead, churches offered a sense of home, a resting and gathering place in the face of an often hostile world. Because of the importance of the church, black Americans still search for the right fit in membership, with personal and communal meaning beyond time spent in the pews on Sunday.

Whether it has involved participation in independent or mainstream churches, black religious life has revolved around a commitment to express the depth of faith. Religion has been part of the creative life of black families, and this dimension of black culture continues. That same creativity in searching for and expressing faith has led to black religious movements. Some grow into formal religions, such as the Eternal Life Christian Spiritualist Church begun in New Orleans under the direction of Mother Leafy Anderson in the early 1920s. This church adopted practices and beliefs from "Roman Catholicism, Pentecostalism, nineteenth-century Spiritualism, New Thought, and African religious concepts that were incorporated into what is known as Voodoo or hoodoo in the United States."[5] Other churches break ties with Christianity, as did the Nation of Islam, which also began in the 1920s with the teachings of Wallace Fard, who claimed that Islam was the original religion of black people. Other African Americans search among religions that stem from traditional African belief systems, such as Afro-Cuban Lukumì or Brazilian Candomblè.

The search for religious fulfillment is an integral part of African American life, giving proof to the importance of the black church in black culture, though the expression of religion has taken many forms. It is to historical understandings that we now turn.

BLACK CHURCH HISTORY: Changing and Staying the Same

Many African Americans claimed their black identities with pride before the American public through the civil rights and black power movements. African Americans' spirituality came through to the wider American public in new and more intense ways as images of black people singing while attacked by fire hoses and dogs appeared on the front pages of morning papers and on television. The American public could see that fiery religious preaching and a similar nonreligious declamation spurred the protesters, and music sustained them.

The ability to inspire social action and develop forms of culture has been part and parcel of the history of black churches. The forms of musical and preaching expressions that came from churches were woven into black American culture and are now part of the religious and nonreligious creative life in black communities. Gospel music, rhythm and blues, comedy styles, politicians' speeches, and some folk expressions are rooted in black church life.

Links such as these between religion and black creative expression are indicators of the central importance of religious life for African Americans. It is no wonder, then, that the black church has long been a focus for African American scholars. I will draw from the works of a few black scholars to demonstrate the historical groundings of today's prosperity churches in the ongoing tensions of black church life.

Three prominent black thinkers—historian Carter G. Woodson, sociologist E. Franklin Frazier, and religion scholar C. Eric Lincoln —have discussed the black church and its developments at different points during the twentieth century. Their studies indicate some important themes as well as point to some effects of historical changes that will bear on the discussion of black prosperity churches.

Carter G. Woodson wrote a history of the Negro church in 1921, less than fifty years after the end of enslavement but with Jim

Crow firmly established. Woodson identified two strands among Negro churches, which he termed conservative and progressive. These two strands, he stated, were traceable back to the end of enslavement when preachers promoted thankfulness to God for freedom—and this, they claimed, was the primary role of the Negro church, creating the first conservative strand. But this view could not last under the influence of education. As black Americans became more educated, a religious diet of thanks, praise, and revelation were not sustaining and not consistent with some of the new ideas that surfaced. The educated black person, therefore, "no longer thought of religion as the panacea for all the ills of the race. . . . There can be little revelation where there is arrested mental development."[6]

From this, Woodson defined the split between conservative and progressive Negro church members in ways that presage the theologies of some prosperity churches:

> The conservatives believed that the individual should sacrifice all for the church. On Sunday, they would come from afar to swell the chorus of the faithful, and there they would remain during the day, leaving their net earnings in the hands of management, given at the cost of a sacrifice placed on a common altar. The educated Negro, on the other hand, thought of the church as existing for the good of the individual. It was to him a means for making the bad good, and if the institution were defective it might be so reshaped and reorganized as to serve the useful purposes of man.[7]

Woodson claimed that the conservative-progressive tensions of his time resulted in some interesting outcomes, which may also be instructive for our time. On the progressive side, he stated, the Negro church was "socialized," meaning that physical and spiritual help was offered so that members could obtain some of the social welfare they needed through their home churches. They aimed to "make the world a decent place to live."[8]

Yet, the conservative strand of church life helped black people to learn what Woodson termed "self-control," which he deemed a spiritual lesson of the church.

> The watchword of the Negro church has been patience while waiting on the Lord. The Negro has learned not to avenge his own

wrongs, believing that God will adjust matters in the end. . . . The Negro is conservatively Christian and looks forward to that favorable turn in the affairs of man when the wrongs of the oppressed shall be righted without the shedding of blood.[9]

The ability to wait kept most black people (recognizing a radical fringe element) from committing socially and politically rash acts, thereby helping them to survive, Woodson declared. He also said that despite this split, because of the centrality of the church in black lives, both conservative and progressive churches became the places white people went to get information to black people.

From this brief look at Woodson's Negro church history, there are several running themes that have meaning today. First of all, what we know of today as the black church has never had a uniform voice. There have consistently been conservative and progressive strands; these we may identify differently for our time, but those strands still exist. This look back at history also identifies the black theological conflict between faith and reason. Because black people have experienced oppression, reconciling our faith beliefs with our realities might become difficult. This quandary can be stated simply with several questions. Do black people wait on God to fix our personal, social, or national problems? Is waiting reasonable for a person of faith? Or is a person of faith required to do something to make changes?

Another important note from Woodson's history is about what he terms the "socialized" church. Blending spiritual life with social and political realities has been a strong strand of black religious life. The actual method of addressing social and political problems in black communities has had a range of answers depending on how the question is framed. Do I seek "to make the world a decent place to live" for my family and myself only? For the neighboring community? For all African Americans? For the United States?

The story that sociologist E. Franklin Frazier told of the Negro church is differently shaped than Woodson's. Forty years after Woodson's *History of the Negro Church*, Frazier's *The Negro Church in America* was published in the United States, in 1964, two years after his death. Frazier's work had some serious flaws, but he also identified several important factors about black churches as centers of social, political, and economic life for black Americans.

For instance, Woodson may have seen the impact of the end of enslavement on black communities, but Frazier identified the influence on churches' structures of black migration from the rural South to urban centers. Frazier noted that as a direct result of urbanization, "Negro cults" and storefront churches had grown and sometimes flourished.[10] More significantly, African Americans in city centers moved into new, sometimes unionized jobs that brought them into more collegial contact with white Americans. "Willy-nilly, Negroes are drawn into the complex social organization of the American community. This is necessary for mere survival."[11] Frazier held up black business as a way to insure social acceptance even as he believed that the middle class distanced themselves from the everyday folkways of lower class black people. Strivings for middle class position and acceptability in wider America created great distances between black people and churches. While Frazier noted that poor black people remained shut out from such class mobility, "they are nevertheless increasingly assimilating the manners and customs of American society. Thus is achieved a certain external conformity to the patterns of American culture."[12] The logical end to Frazier's argument is that eventually black people would be fully assimilated into the mainstream of America by a kind of social attrition.

Frazier's idea of the possibilities of assimilation was also based on his contention that Africans retained none of their original cultural understandings, that these were lost through the experiences of enslavement. "In the New World the process by which the Negro was stripped of his social heritage and thereby, in a sense, dehumanized was completed."[13] Following this erroneous line of thought, Frazier was able to reach other conclusions and criticisms about black life and the importance of religion.

For instance, he contrasts black family life and sexual behavior during and after enslavement. During enslavement, the "Negro family was essentially an amorphous group gathered around the mother or some female on the plantation."[14] The biological father was unimportant under enslavement; "he might disappear as the result of the sale of slaves or because of a whimsical change of his own feelings or affection." However, Frazier notes "family and sex relations were constantly under the supervision of Whites." The white supervision seems to have made a significant difference in Frazier's way of thinking; he sees the contrast following enslavement as a cause for moral decay. "The removal of the authority of masters . . . caused promiscuous sex relations to become widespread and permitted the constant changing of spouses."[15] Negro churches became the safeguard against moral decline by educating members to take their places within existing structures of already freed black communities—who had more closely aligned themselves with European mores. Churches also supported the "patriarchal family to be found in the Bible"[16] and found other ways, such as leadership development, to bolster the family position of black men. Ultimately, Frazier states, "The churches undertook as organizations to censure unconventional and immoral sex behavior and to punish by expulsion sex offenders and those who violated monogamous mores."[17]

The issues around black churches and social control of the behavior of members overlap into discussions of today's prosperity churches. The connections will be seen in a later chapter but it is important to note now that churches have often assumed powerful roles that shape members' behaviors since they have been the fundamental, long-standing institutions throughout the history of black American communities. Frazier's discussion highlights how marriage, family, and sexuality were promoted in ways that, ultimately, would bring about greater assimilation of black people into white value systems and, therefore, greater participation in American society.[18]

C. Eric Lincoln, a preeminent scholar of black religion, published *The Black Church Since Frazier*[19] in the same volume as *The Negro Church*. Lincoln identified sweeping social and political changes effected since Frazier's analysis, including civil rights and black power movements, along with the growth of black theology and the Nation of Islam. "The Negro Church accepted death in order to be reborn. Out of the ashes of its funeral pyre there sprang the bold, strident, self-conscious phoenix that is the contemporary black Church."[20] Lincoln saw the black church as radically distinct from the Negro church, "a conscious departure from the critical norms which made the Negro Church what it was."[21] The social changes resulting from the struggles for human rights and the basic recognition of black humanity shaped a radical shift as churches became definite instruments of freedom, according to Lincoln. This was not easily accomplished nor was it a simple decision, but it stood in contrast to the conservative strand of the black church, a strand that Woodson had already noted in the 1920s. Lincoln pointed out the conservative strand thusly: "The notion of white invincibility and black vulnerability and contingency, the suspicion of black leadership, the concerns for the white man's soul and for the divine prerogative to initiate change—all add up to a basic, inherent conservatism."[22] Lincoln noted, however, that these features stood to assist the black Christian church in the development of a "mature religious posture" that retained a religious identification and spiritual direction rather than becoming solely focused on social activism.

There were historic developments in black church life between Woodson and Frazier and significant social changes between Frazier and Lincoln. The black church had its historical tensions, some of which were pointed out by scholars such as Woodson, Frazier, and Lincoln: conservative versus progressive, urban versus rural, the elite versus the masses, and assimilation to white versus retention of black cultural patterns. These and other tensions have continually brewed and bubbled up in different forms in black communities' churches. Some of these same tensions will be seen in other forms in the discussions about black prosperity churches. But new things occur as well. Since C. Eric Lincoln penned his words, the breadth and depth of social and religious changes have been astonishing.

INTO THE PRESENT: Sociocultural Changes and Black Churches

Prosperity churches in black communities tie into the history presented by the three aforementioned authors by seeming to provide answers to questions that have lingered throughout the history: Conservative or progressive churches? Gratify self or work for the betterment of society? Stress family and middle-class values? Find more ways to assimilate into American society? The answers prosperity preaching provides and their multileveled impact will be further discussed throughout the book. But before turning to these expressions, we need to look toward the realities of black church life, in conjunction with and expressed through cultural forms.

Culture is both process and its products. It is a process because what we think of as a given culture grows and develops over time as people interact with meanings. It is its products because we most often recognize "culture" when expressions such as music or art are completed. There are obvious places where African American cultural expressions in conjunction with religion can be noted. For example, spirituals were one form of worship song, but black people continued to create and gospel was born. Gospel music itself is not a single form; for instance, Sister Rosetta Tharpe in the 1930s sounds very different from Mahalia Jackson in the 1950s. Differences stand in sharp relief when the contemporary styling of Yolanda Adams is compared with either of the earlier singers. Regardless of these style changes, each performer seeks to employ the cultural forms of her time in worship. For most African Americans, the sacred is expressed in the daily experiences of human life and so cultural adaptations occur as political, economic, educational, and social conditions change.

Since the 1960s, social conditions have led to extended reflections on what it means to claim a religious faith and be black in America. This reflection was critical for black Christians since, as Lincoln pointed out, black power and religious movements such as the Nation of Islam were critical of the black church's responses to the oppressions of the past. Yet the black church has been an integral part of African American life, and during this same time period, civil rights activities were informed by some black churches and black cultural religious styles—such as gospel singing—that aided protesters by strengthening their resolve to continue.

During this same timeframe of the 1960s, black theology developed, with the life experiences of black people at the center of its discussions. The focus included the scholarly analysis of African Americans' experiences of oppression as well as the methods we have used to overcome them in light of faith. From these analyses, theological statements about black religious meaning could be made. In the 1970s, preeminent black theologian James Cone provided an example when he noted some distinctive features of black prayer: "In black prayer the soul is laid bare before the Lord. All pretensions of goodness are rejected before what the people call 'the throne of grace.'

It was a form of self-criticism not derived from the value system of white people."[23] In this brief excerpt, Cone identified black prayer expressions and contrasted them with white American value systems. In such a manner, black religious scholars such as Cone, Cain Hope Felder, Jacquelyn Grant, and Katie Geneva Cannon began building a body of knowledge about African American theologies and ethics that has grown over the years.

Even as black religious scholars were finding ways to tell the stories of African American faith, the social and cultural changes across the wider American landscape continued. Civil rights and voting rights acts seemed to signal new opportunities. Black power concepts seemed to point the way to strong black pride. Later, affirmative action programs seemed to signal that the United States had begun to sincerely embrace its black population. But conflicts were inherent to the hopes of integration.

Integration brought new, conflicting opportunities. Educational expectations were still tempered by television images and personal experiences of racist efforts to resist integrating schools. Long court battles ensued in the North as well as the South over bussing black children to formerly white schools. Buying homes in white neighborhoods that were better than some segregated areas became a reality for many African Americans who sought to improve their living conditions. The conflicts black families encountered that came from education and new home ownership were beautifully portrayed by the Lorraine Hansberry play *Raisin in the Sun*. Even as black Americans struggled with new realities, white Americans (who could afford it) were moving to other neighborhoods and enrolling their children in private schools, thereby defining a new form of racial segregation.

There had been hope in most black and some white American communities for social changes that would end the American racial divide. But ending legal segregation provided no easy answers for white or black Americans. The civil rights movement did not yield simple answers for black communities. The consciousness-raising efforts of black power workers did not result in all African Americans embracing their racial identities. The next chapter will explore in more detail socioeconomic changes that occurred after the 1960s that subsequently altered meanings of religion and cultural expression for black communities and individuals. First, however, we consider some ways that the black church as an institution has been reshaped in interaction with American culture. This reshaping will also have a direct relationship to prosperity preaching.

MARKETING BLACK RELIGION

The past has taken on new meanings with the seismic shifts in black church life, for example, the volcanic shift felt by my elderly aunt in the phenomenon of megachurches. The streams within history of such forces as civil rights and black power movements, combined with cultural changes such as the Internet and hip hop music, have converged to reshape the twenty-first-century black church. There is perhaps no greater sign of the changes to contemporary society than marketing.

Everything is marketed today, making access to goods and services appear easy to acquire. Television, radio, and print media have been technologically enhanced to make programs easier to watch or hear, while at the same time other technologies have improved recording and receiving information. Marketing specialists know how to target groups by age, race, or gender so advertisements are more effective than ever before because of their specificity. The effect of advertising on our lives is tremendous. Lives can be directed and influenced by media, with television sets often in each of the main rooms of a home. The times when a program or sporting event will be aired become times that meetings are not scheduled because attendees "have to" find a place to watch it. One example is Super Bowl Sunday, when championship football is played. Many churches will limit the length of the services so that members can get ready for the game. Marketing makes it appear to Americans that we live in a "golden age" where all is possible and everything can be had for the right price. If a person does not have the money now, he or she can get it via many forms of credit, or perhaps by gambling with lottery and casino games, each one marketed to nurture the monetary hopes and dreams of poorer community members.

Marketing has been both the means and the ends through which reshaping has occurred, and some churches have begun their own marketing campaigns. For example, there are many billboards that advertise to black congregations. The billboards are common today across the United States in urban areas with significant African American populations: a black man and woman—pastor and wife or bishop and wife/pastor—smile across highways to invite potential members to visit their Christian church. The photos are posed so that the man is in a position of dominance, the wife placed perhaps behind him, or off center. On rare occasions, billboards show a black woman preacher, but without a corresponding man beside her.

Sometimes, the billboard holds a single male or female figure, the action photo taken in a preaching or singing mode. These types of billboards are often advertisements for a particular event, such as a conference; the sole figure is usually a well-known gospel artist. In these ads, the viewer is invited to come and experience something personally uplifting and exhilarating that ultimately promotes a particular denomination. However many ways these billboards are arranged, they intend to invite the viewer to a church, a home, and security.

The groups able to afford billboards do not represent all black churches; yet the dominance of advertising piety in these public forums creates a social climate that feeds some churches and starves others. Therefore, commercialization becomes a survival ploy for many black church groups, with some practices adopted even by small congregations.

If marketing becomes a means to get people into the church, it can also become an end in itself. In some black churches, members are bombarded with advertisements of products for sale in the church. Some of the largest black churches are self-enclosed business entities, offering womb-to-tomb services, sometimes for sale, sometimes only for the benefit of the dues-paid members: day care, educational programs, schools, travel clubs or agencies, senior citizen housing, and funeral homes. Some of larger black churches even offer the services of lawyers so that members can leave a bequest to the church.

None of these are unique to black communities; white churches have been involved in such business practices as well. Many of these practices are readily identifiable with those in the white megachurches. Religious marketing has been occurring in other forms as well. The traveling revival can trace its roots back to

American Great Awakenings and evangelicalism. But it took the genius of Billy Graham to shape the revival into a well-marketed machine that attracted millions of believers to his ministry. His use of television and radio, city-to-city tours, and books and pamphlets became the template for many other types of religious marketing. For African American communities, participation in religious marketing practices is a sign of the sweep toward religious commodification.

If black religion can be seen as part of black cultural patterns, the drive toward commodification is not surprising. Commodifying aspects of black cultural life has been an American sport that has largely benefited white business people. Sale of black culture began during enslavement as black people grew the rice or the cotton, made the bricks, and wove the cloth by drawing from their own cultures to achieve the tasks for which white people took credit. Entertainment, particularly the music industry, would never have achieved a uniquely *American* sound without the contributions and often leadership of African Americans. Many other American styles of dance, dress, and speech can be traced to black cultural patterns. But the simple extraction of cultural information is not the whole story.

The mammy stereotype provides an example. White people did not understand black women's culturally derived nurturing patterns and such misunderstandings came to inform black-white domestic relationships during and after enslavement. White people saw dark women, desexualized the women, and interpreted their behavior as "wanting" to take care of "their" white folk. Black women's nurturing patterns were then caricatured. The Aunt Jemima mascot was clearly a mammy figure; it was also a most successful advertising campaign. Although the figure has been updated, it has not disappeared and continues to sell pancake batter. This is a case where the commodification of a black cultural pattern—specifically a form of nurturing—is extended to the objectification of the black body. Turning black cultural patterns into commodities that can be sold on the market will include selling black bodies or body parts in some form. In these ways, black culture is dissected from African Americans' intellectual work and black faces are used to sell the products.

Until the last twenty years, African Americans have been in a strange and uncomfortable relationship when producing our own culture for marketing. Madame C. J. Walker became rich in the nineteenth century selling hair products to meet black women's needs. Today, majority white-owned conglomerates have captured the black hair product market, controlling quality, sales, and development. As black people historically became the means to white earnings, money has both broken and created racial barriers in this country. Even as black faces were used as sales gimmicks, the humanness of those same people was questioned. The result has been a precise exclusion of black people from creating our own public images and marketing ourselves, simultaneously limiting any profits that can accrue to black communities.

But churches remain the primary organizations that are owned and operated by black people. Members' sense of ownership and pride in their church homes is fierce. The level of commitment is interwoven into daily life, and so church has been more than just a place to visit on Sundays. The centrality of church life means that, as an institution, social customs and mores have grown in these settings. While formats may change from church to church, the sense of being connected to a larger community grouping becomes one of the important reasons that people join one or another congregation. For this reason, the billboards previously mentioned have great invitational power as black people seek a church home where they can be comfortable.

Besides marketing their specific congregations to community members, black entrepreneurs have learned to market African American religious styles and messages. Morality and life lessons are taught, while certain values are upheld in these marketing efforts. Moral lessons—such as the reasons to remain faithful in a marriage—offer ideas about applying religious ideas in daily life. Artistic performance is the usual way such messages are delivered, gospel music and praise dancing being primary forms that attract the participation of church members. Praise fests and choir competitions featuring local talent are sometimes held in cities with significant black populations. These everyday events have developed into black entertainment networks in which religious-themed stage plays tour the country. Some of these plays have achieved wild success, such as plays by Tyler Perry. Perry cross-dresses and plays a black woman—Madea—who offers folksy wisdom and life lessons with mildly religious themes.

The marketing of African American religions today signifies something new about the state of what is termed the black church. Regardless of these changes, there are cultures, societies, and communication patterns developed within black churches. These are social structures that provide other dimensions to understanding prosperity preaching in black communities.

SOCIAL STRUCTURES IN BLACK CHURCHES

Relationships and roles that develop in black churches reflect the cultural and historical perspectives of African Americans. This would seem to be obvious, but it is not always clear. It becomes clear when a black group is part of a church with a majority white population. Often, in what I believe is an attempt at fairness on the part of the white members, the expectation is that the black families will be just like "us." The statement that "I don't see your color, I see *you*" at first glance may seem to be a welcoming statement. But it hides many levels of American social problems. The comment renders the black person invisible. It implies that the real problems arising from racism will never be addressed because race itself is denied. Further, the black person is bound never to raise criticism based on race because that would be deemed divisive. The statement also indicates that, ultimately, nothing will ever change because we are caught in a polite facade that denies race and racism.

But in our prayer lives, if we are honest, the reality of who we are must be addressed. To worship without bringing our entire selves, including experiences, is entering into the ultimate dishonest relationship. Prayer may change things, but it does not erase them. Black Americans bring a black culturally conditioned awareness into worship as people of other cultures and ethnicities bring theirs. These fully engaged worship experiences enrich, rather than limit, our prayer lives.

The distinctive experiences of African Americans are expressed in their religious lives, hence, the virtual reality of the black church and its real significance in black communities. Looking at prosperity preaching in black communities will bring several of these unique aspects of black religious life into view.

There are three categories that are important in this exploration. The first category is worship and ritual, including where black cultural expression is employed in structured prayer. The second is the shared identity and meaning that comprise a church community. The third category is social construction, the day-to-day operations that outline the community's morality and memory. Each of these areas is grounded in a theological base. Each is constructed with deliberation. Part of the interesting story of prosperity churches is how and who assembles these three areas.

There is one more perspective needed before specifically exploring prosperity churches in black communities—that of black communities in light of the meaning of prosperity and why it is so important to black religious life.

A SPIRITUALITY OF LONGING

I f my aunt's ideas about church led me to think about the present and past black church, my visits to several black churches where theologies of prosperity are preached from the pulpit and enacted in the pews brought me to another set of questions. Why are black Americans drawn to these churches? Certainly, African Americans are religiously creative people, to which any student of black religious history could attest. If there were but a few prosperity churches, they would only be evidence of this creativity. However, there is more than creativity happening as prosperity preaching influences other facets of black church life. I visited several of these churches and spoke with their members. I did not seek out the leadership of these churches; rather, I wanted to know some stories of congregation members and to experience the worship. I kept circling back to the question: why are black Americans drawn to these church communities? This chapter explores this question and the answers I discovered.

Longing, I believe, has always been a significant component of black American spirituality. This *longing* signifies a story that is internal to black communities, the result of African American experiences within the context of the economy of the United States.

BLACK ECONOMIC LIFE IN THE UNITED STATES (since the 1960s)

Perhaps nothing has been so momentous in shaping black Americans' economic life today than the fact that they were brought to the colonies that would become the United States as unpaid labor. Enslaved, these people lived under unjust state, federal, and local legal systems that granted them little status and no human rights. While legal enslavement ended in the 1860s, it was reconstituted through Jim Crow practices as legalities again circumscribed black humanity.

With the mid-twentieth century laws that ended disenfranchisement in voting and segregation in schools, with the promises of equal opportunity and equal pay came hopes that black and white inequality would be remedied. Some African Americans did indeed benefit economically from these social changes and the black middle-class sector increased. Since the 1960s and the seeming gains from the civil rights and black power movements, there have been many Americans who believe the impact of centuries of unpaid laboring should be ignored or forgotten, that we should become "one" country instead of one divided by discussions of black oppressions and the effects of racism. This would be a noble sentiment if not for the ways that racism and accompanying economic inequities have been reconstituted in the early twenty-first century. Several convergent sets of events have created our current realities.

Politically, the loss of black Americans' alliances with liberal whites began by the mid-1960s as white Democrats sought to hold their party together. Tracing the tone of the public arguments on race through such politicians as Lyndon Johnson and Daniel Moynihan, sociologist Stephen Steinberg encapsulates the ideas as follows:

> The liberal retreat from race was rationalized in terms of realpolitik. The arguments ran like this: America is too racist to support programs targeted for blacks, especially if these involve any form of preference, which is anathema to most whites. Highlighting racial issues, therefore, only serves to drive a wedge in the liberal coalition, driving whites from the Democratic Party. . . . The liberal backlash was not based on racial animus or retrograde politics. On the contrary, these dyed-in-the-wool liberals were convinced that the best or only way to help blacks was to help everybody.[1]

Race became a topic causing white Americans, especially, to be uncomfortable and therefore avoided. Today, despite the past history of struggles, race is itself poorly understood by the American public. This ignorance serves to perpetuate social inequities. As defined by social historian Manning Marable:

Race is a dynamic, changing social relationship grounded in structural inequality. As the human composition of American society's social order has shifted, the lived reality of structural racism has also changed in everyday existence. What has remained constant, unfortunately, is that "blackness," no matter how it is constituted in ethnic terms, has continued to be stigmatized and relegated to the periphery of power and opportunity.[2]

The result of a social trajectory that denies race or racism can be seen clearly in the twenty-first century. The general social climate in which we live furthers the myth that many Americans accept about what it means to be citizens in the United States. The myth centers on equality and opportunity for everyone who "works hard." For most African Americans, though, the myth is quickly destroyed by the realities of daily life. Programs such as affirmative action, which were established to end the effects of segregation, are no longer deemed politically viable by politicians today.

If there are political dimensions, there are also economic dimensions. Economist Marcellus Andrews critically analyzes the current economic situation for black Americans. The current system of free market capitalism, through which, allegedly, anyone who works hard can succeed, operates on several principles that are crippling to many black Americans. Savings and investments are important for growing the American economy, but black Americans have been under- and unpaid labor for an extended period of time, and it is only within the last fifty years that opportunities to amass wealth have been open to them. Therefore, there has been no significant accumulation of wealth in black communities, certainly nothing parallel to that of white communities. Experience is prized as one key to increasing productivity under free market ideologies. Because black Americans historically have been shut out of several fields, they could not obtain the long-term experience considered necessary for job advancement.

To adapt to changing work environments, education has been important.

A highly educated work force that has extensive experience with rapidly changing technologies, and that can pass on knowledge of how to succeed in academic competition to its children, will be able to improve its ability to work over time, quite apart from any investments in new types of machines and production methods.[3]

But black Americans have had unequal access to education as part of "the considerable legacy of historic underinvestment in the human capital of blacks."[4]

This confluence of economic factors has become market driven segregation "as middle-class whites used their high incomes to demand economic and social distance from blacks" and, Andrews concludes, the result is nothing more than free market racism.[5]

These ideas are backed up by a variety of statistical data. For instance, in November 2006, the unemployment rate for white Americans was 3.9 percent and for black Americans 8.6 percent.[6] Fields that are expected to grow are health care, education, and professional and business services, all of which require access to higher education.[7] Giving the numbers meaning in the daily life of many black people, Manning Marable stated: "The new racial domain is constructed as a deadly triangle (or perhaps an 'unholy trinity') of structural racism: mass unemployment, mass incarceration, and mass disenfranchisement. . . . The cycle of destruction starts with chronic, mass unemployment and poverty."[8]

The situations in New Orleans following hurricane Katrina are more commonly known and provide excellent examples of ways black and poor communities are systematically shorted. But there are other examples of systematic underinvestment in and disenfranchisement of black communities, such as the plight of black farmers. Loans and political supports through the United States Department of Agriculture (USDA) are what hold up farming, in general, as important to society. And although there has certainly been erosion of all individual or family ownership of farms in light of the corporatization of farming as large companies take over agriculture, the American image of a "farmer" is white. The average U.S. farmer's income—propped up by regulations and loans—was eighty thousand dollars in 2005.[9] This has not been the experience of black farmers, who have fallen between the cracks of social and financial supports. The lack of such supports exacerbates the erosion of black farmland ownership.

Black farmers won a class action lawsuit against the USDA in 1998 (Pigford v. Glickman), following decades of systematic denial of equal opportunity for loans and support that white farmers had received. In the opinion issued by U.S. District Judge Paul L. Friedman, the relationship of black Americans with the land has consistently been weakened. Friedman traces the history of black land loss to the period following the Civil War. "By 1920, there were 925,000 African American farms in the United States. . . . Today, there are fewer than 18,000 African American farms."[10] Yet the National Black Farmers' Association has proven that the USDA has avoided paying out the settlement using a variety of obstructionist methods. Less than half of eligible farmers have received the payment of fifty thousand dollars; most have been denied. The situation of black farmers is only one instance of the constant assault against African Americans. While ropes and dogs may not be used today, corporations and courts are equally effective methods of denying black people in the United States.

Many white Americans prefer to take no responsibility for these situations. After all, a young white student in one of my classes stated angrily, "Why should we give *them* something *they* haven't worked for?" Feminist anthropologist Micaela di Leonardo addresses many of the myths about black people's inability to parent or lead wholesome lives, concluding:

> Most minorities are much poorer than most Whites—kept poorer by the concatenation of tens of thousands of individual White actions that maintain the condition despite often valiant efforts to escape. And it's also true that poverty encourages family discord and channels criminal tendencies toward the street. You don't get many chances to run million-dollar white-collar scams from the projects."[11]

LOOKING FOR DEAD PRESIDENTS

By no means have African Americans been passive in the face of their economic oppressions. During the Jim Crow era and legal segregation, black Americans began businesses ranging from boarding houses to newspapers to funeral homes to meet their communities' needs. Black business associations were begun, which aided growth. These black businesses were not as elegant or well financed as were most white businesses. So when segregated facilities were outlawed through various legislations of the 1960s and 1970s, black businesses were often unable to compete with similar white businesses. Despite the changes in this landscape, as sociologist Robert Weems argues, companies and their advertising campaigns have given black Americans little respect as the significance of the black consumer dollar has grown.

> It is clear that, since the passage of the Civil Rights Act of 1964 . . . individual African Americans possess more consumer goods than ever before. Still, if one were to take a stroll through most urban black enclaves in America, one would be hard pressed to see where increased African American spending has improved the infrastructure and the ambiance of these neighborhoods. Black consumers, who now spend the vast majority of their money in shiny downtown and suburban shopping malls, enhance the economic bases of these outside areas to the detriment of their own enclaves. . . . A truly free people possess the power to produce as well as to consume.[12]

Even as black Americans have watched families and children and friends struggle in a society that offers few economic incentives, efforts to improve our economic lives continue. Money plays an important role in African American life, especially today. Most of us are wage earners; a few of us are business owners. Very few of us are independently wealthy, most of us live paycheck to paycheck. The pressures to have and get money create untold stress every day and, as one researcher stated, "It is no surprise that in a society where financial success often determines individuals' sense of worth, financial stress is negatively associated with the self-esteem of African Americans."[13] Now this comment is no surprise to most black folks. Our economic lives have generally been controlled through lower wages, higher prices for just about everything, and limited local access to quality goods.

Most African Americans recognize that the twentieth century offered new opportunities for economic growth and most have sought a route to accessing some financial gain. The black American push toward fulfilling the Horatio-Alger myth of success has new proponents. The titles of three books written by black authors in the

1990s and geared for the general public tell the story: "*Why Should White Guys Have All the Fun?*": *How Reginald Lewis Created a Billion Dollar Business Empire,*[14] *How to Succeed in Business without Being White,*[15] and *Think and Grow Rich: A Black Choice.*[16] Each of these books downplays racism's effects. Each book encourages entrepreneurship in such a way that it addresses the black longing for success in the United States.

But the terms for the success are not set by these authors from their experiences; rather, they are drawn exactly from the capitalistic framework that has created the injustices experienced by black people. Equating success with money and reducing values to those of a capitalistic culture seems to be a similar motivation for many thug rappers today. That the only judgment for success is in the number of dollars decorated with pictures of "dead presidents" is infused into the songs of many rappers. Selling drugs and "pimping" are held out as viable ways to get money. For some black Americans today, "by any means necessary" refers to getting as many dead presidents as possible in any way they can. The media-produced culture of rap music, videos, and thug life styles (financed in the main by white businesses) provide young black people with ideas about the value of money and success in America. These images come at a time when too many black parents may not be able to direct their children in a mass culture in which they themselves are immersed.

Compounding this, for the most part, there was no communal or familial knowledge from which African Americans could draw that directly related to the new experiences. During the 1970s, there were businesses from which black people had been legally excluded—everything from restaurants to clothing stores—where we had to learn how to act or react. There were agencies—from hospitals to government offices—where we had to decipher the levels of service we did or did not receive. Access to higher education brought its own set of stressors, where we had to more intimately interact with people who often tried to treat us as if we were invisible. Black families were expected to become more like white Americans, to stop being "angry" and wholeheartedly practice patriarchy. Some black families succeeded and arrived at middle-class status. Yet, this often resulted in brand new class stratification that then set black people against each other. There are middle-class African Americans who are working to change black communities. But moving away from the discord of poverty is a pleasant option only for those with the money to do so.

Dealing with these complex realities over the years may have resulted in what philosopher Cornel West terms "black nihilism" or "the profound sense of psychological depression, personal worthlessness, and social despair so widespread in black America."[17] If nothing else, his term becomes a kind of wake-up call for African Americans to rethink who we are in the United States. Whether or not one agrees with West's assessment, the veracity of black levels of stress and despair caused by social and economic situations today cannot be denied.

Substantive thinking about African Americans' economic realities is being done. The National Urban League, which has over one hundred affiliate offices throughout the United States, annually publishes *The State of Black America* report. Beginning in 2004, the report began to include the "Equality Index," which measures the status of black people in five areas: economics, health, education, social justice, and civic engagement. In the 2005 report, Urban League President Marc Morial stated,

> [O]ur inaugural *Equality Index* determined the status of black Americans to be 0.73 of their fellow white Americans . . . a stunning indication of the glacial pace of the progress America has made toward equal opportunity in the century and a half since the end of the Civil War, the emancipation of blacks from slavery, and the constitutional correction, via the Thirteenth Amendment, of the wrong of the three-fifths clause [which legally defined a black slave as three fifths of a person].[18]

The economics index was made up of five indicators: median income, poverty rates, employment issues, housing and wealth formation, and access to technology, or the digital divide. The Equality Index number for economics alone in 2005 was 0.57. "This low index number means blacks are performing disproportionately worse than whites in economic criteria."[19]

The National Urban League may offer programs through many of its affiliate offices, but radio and TV personality Tavis Smiley, in his widely promoted book *The Covenant with Black America* also offers social, including economic, remedies for black Americans' consideration. Smiley coordinated black leaders across the United States in developing the book. In the introduction, Smiley states the book's intent to emphasize the multicultural and multiracial nature of the United States.

> Now is the time to make real the promises of our democracy. Now is the time—from health to housing, crime to criminal justice, education to economic parity—to transform these devastating disparities to hope and healing. . . . I believe when we make black America better, we make all America better.[20]

The ten chapters deal with topics such as home ownership, improving education, and accessing good jobs and wealth. Each chapter lists relevant data about the topic; distinguishes what individuals, communities, and leaders can do to address issues; and highlights organizations or practices that are successful in creating remedies.

Both *The Covenant with Black America* and *The State of Black America* are distinctly different from the popular grow-rich-like-white-folks books. Both the Urban League and Smiley books analyze race and racism's impact, even as they promote ways to counter negative social situations. They both promote ideas that will work through, not ignore, current conditions. However, the grow-rich books may be more popular. After all, they seem to offer easier, less painful solutions, and the cover of each of these is graced with a slick photo of a smiling, prosperous looking black man. While economic inequities can begin to be addressed through programs, these will take time. As the Urban League's 2005 report states, the equality index for African Americans is still 0.73.

The situation of black churches is another layer in the economic story of black Americans providing no clear answers. Churches in black communities may not be able to provide leadership to address the social issues. Some black churches themselves are struggling financially to keep the doors open. Some black denominations are shaped by a theology that emphasizes the spiritual dimensions to the exclusion of physical needs. Other churches have no idea how to deal with black middle-class struggles. As scholars develop theologies and theories about the black church, individual churches' members are being drawn into new relationships in work, school, and society—the same new relationships with which some black pastoral staff are trying to cope themselves. Running like a strong current under black Americans' religious lives, a spirituality of longing has been shaped by our economic realities.

A SPIRITUALITY OF LONGING

Spirituality is a word too often limited to referencing those things that are not physical, to things or persons related to ministry, or to the values of a given denomination. The problem with these definitions is that they narrow the possibilities of spirituality, which is a fully human experience that may include the body, emotions, mind, and something beyond those. It may be experienced individually or with others. For instance, one woman told me that the most spiritual experience she ever had was at a concert of the great jazz organist Jimmy Smith. Someone else mentioned an out-of-body experience after viewing an art show. Another woman told me of the shared spiritual experience of an entire audience after one of the last concert performances of Ray Charles. Spirituality is not controlled by any denomination or religious tradition, although each organized religion can identify its own unique flavor of encountering and defining the spiritual. Yet atheists may have a particular spirituality. Spirituality may be tied to a Divine Being or it may be tied to the earth. Spirituality is experienced and recognized in different ways over a person's lifetime. Because humans experience it, spirituality will necessarily reflect cultures and nationalities and gender and class. Spirituality is a way of being in the world.

With this broad working definition, it is appropriate to think about how spirituality might be defined in African American contexts. Flora Bridges is a pastor who defines African American spirituality as a "source of resilience in their struggle for the freedom of self-determination [and] as the triumph of good . . . in the face of overwhelming evil."[21] Black theologian Dwight Hopkins defines spirituality so as to encompass African American as well as other people's ideas: "A belief in an ultimate power greater than any individual person that is embedded in the textures and contours of specific human cultures, collective and individual selves, and sociologically and phenotypically determined races."[22] Leslie King-Hammond takes another view and considers the multiple ways that spirituality is expressed in African American art. She states that, from the time black people were brought to the colonies, they had

> an imperative need to locate *safe* space—a *sacred* and often secret space to protect the Africans' spiritual identity and when necessary their physical state of well-being. . . . Visioning and representing a religious imagery for these new Africanized American communities of geographically and ethnically "scrambled" Africans demanded a process of *re*-vision and *re*-presentation.[23]

Each of these views of spirituality turns toward a holistic cosmology, which does not separate the body from the spirit or the person from the community. This holistic view creates interconnected experience, so that the spiritual can be expressed in physical space, demonstrated through culture, and shared, thereby becoming a defining moment for people in a community. Spirituality is indeed a way of being human in the world.

For African Americans, life in the United States was fraught with danger, and longing became one way of envisioning something beyond a given reality. Enslavement was a period when African Americans longed for freedom; this longing was expressed in prayer, in song, in quilts, and in dance. Christianity, the historic religious tradition of most black Americans, was a lens through which enslavement and its many injustices were viewed and found inhumane. The biblical images of the Exodus story that resulted in the Hebrew slaves freed through God's direct intervention offered hopes and dreams to the enslaved Africans.

The years after the Emancipation Proclamation were still marked by black folks' longing for freedom and acceptance in an unwelcoming country. The civil rights movement attempted to alleviate some of this longing and many remedies were set into motion. However, as we saw in the preceding sections, the possibility for fully ending racial oppression was aborted by the convergence of multiple forces of politics and economics.

An example of the use of artistic forms to communicate this longing is found in the novelist Alice Walker's response to hearing the musical group, Sweet Honey in the Rock, in 1978.

> Sweet Honey's music . . . is inoculation against poison, immunization against the disease of racist and sexist selfishness, envy, and greed. By now my heart had reached my solar plexus, and when I heard the old songs from my grandmother's Hardshell Baptist Church ring out as the freedom songs they always were, I heard all the connectedness that racist oppression and colonial destruction tried to keep hidden. . . . These songs said: We do not come from people who have had nothing. We come rather from people who've had everything—except money, except political power, except freedom. . . . Yes, the singers said, it is not over yet. For we are still captive! Look at the lies, the evasions, the distortions of truth with which we live our lives.[24]

Black Americans have experienced longing in some form throughout time in the United States. Longing might be expressed in myriad ways and not just for economic participation and success. However, financial realities bespeak the sets of relationships that African Americans have experienced with the dominant culture. Work, seemingly prized in the value system of the United States, has provided painful sets of experiences for civil rights movements. Black people do not just long for work, but for meaningful work for which they are justly compensated. African Americans have consistently been forced to the sidelines as others prospered from the fruits of their labor. Black people have been forced to do menial and hard labor, yet not given credit for the genius that served to build the country. To be denied credit and affirmation for one's work is to be denied humanity. This is truly a form of marginalizing black people.

But marginalization has not ended, despite media reports to the contrary. Today, it is more difficult than ever for black people to receive the education needed for advancement, as Manning Marable points out.

> The trends of exclusion and isolation for a new generation for black schoolchildren were so deep and profound that even Rod Paige, George W. Bush's conservative Secretary of Education, was forced

to acknowledge them. 'We face an emerging de facto apartheid in our schools, a contemporary crisis that is similar, perhaps identical, to the situation in the 1950s South," Paige declared in 2004.[25]

When normal roads are closed and social exclusion is normative, it would follow that people still long to achieve success and social acceptance. Therefore, it is no wonder that many young black people are drawn to the communality of gangs and the glamour of thug life.

Control and autonomy are missing from most black Americans' lives, exemplified by the disenfranchisement enacted through the presidential elections of 2000, womanist ethicist Emilie Townes declares. Her statements indicate another longing expressed by many other African Americans.

> In what spaces in this country, then, do black peoples and our kin have control and autonomy? Most of us are barely in control of our lives and we have almost no control over our commodified bodies. Autonomy is a far away ideal. . . . When black identity is property that can be owned by someone else, defined by someone else, created by someone else, shaped by someone else, and marketed by someone else, we are chattel dressed in postmodern silks and linens.[26]

All these forms of what I term *longing* can also be understood as spiritual strivings and fall under the umbrella of a desire for justice.[27] Christianity, after all, is a religion based on a covenantal promise with a God who is understood as all loving. Black lives that are enrolled in a regular regimen of confusion and pain need a spirituality that imbues hope in the promises and makes sense of the inconsistencies. Even so, some black people may turn from religious language because of the inconsistencies between black lives and covenantal promise. But more black people critique the American experiment as lacking in humaneness and moral rectitude; stated simply, God did not create white people or the U.S. social structure to be racist.

Re-visioning the cognitive dissonances that occur between lived realities and the promise of American society has been part of the task of black preachers. Cècile Coquet studied black sermons and identified the concept of God as a "time-God." She drew several ideas from these sermons, highlighting a sermon by Reverend C. L.

Franklin recorded in 1984; Franklin was a powerful preacher in Detroit during his lifetime. Coquet concluded:

> It is quite a shock for anyone expecting to find hope at the heart of every single folk sermon in the African American tradition. Even conversion, towards which every sermon tends, does not appear as being ultimately separated from the central theme of effort or perseverance. The questions of divine promise (covenant) and the certainty of election are no longer posed in terms of immediacy or delay. The promise kept by the preaching is that of solace-giving, a form of spiritual healing giving the chosen people the means to hold on in the wilderness, in a parallel temporal dimension, situated both out of the time of threat and out of the time of justification.[28]

The idea of holding on in the quest for justice is not an accident, according to the analysis of religious historian Larry Murphy. Instead, it is tied to the concept of mission, which has three parts. The first part is the obvious desire to evangelize, and this is more clearly reflected in black Protestant Christian denominations. The second part is the joyous celebration of the wonderful works of God, which is related to the third part:

> [T]he mission of the Black church has been human liberation, particularly focused on Black people, though not exclusive of any others. A sense of mission understood in this manner is pervasive among Black congregations and denominations across the board. . . . One should not expect that every or even most Black congregations are socially activist, only that most at some level will resonate positively with the notion of the church as a legitimate agent in the pursuit of the abundant life, the life of social righteousness and equity for all peoples.[29]

Murphy is not referring to God's abundance as it is used in prosperity theology, as will be explored in later chapters. Instead, he is referring to abundance as a strong biblical image that was emphasized in African American religion long before prosperity preachers came along. For instance, Jesus' parable of the talents (Matt. 25:14–30) instructs Christians in the right use of gifts, which are not to be hoarded and lost but multiplied; the consequences for loss are exclusion from God's own presence. This parable could be narrowly interpreted as promoting investment schemes that give the greatest yield of money. Such an interpretation confines the meanings of the "talents" to God's direct blessing of free market capitalism. But in Matthew's gospel, this parable is followed by a vision of the last judgment of each human, based on what was done for the "least": the sick, the hungry, the stranger, or the prisoner. (Matt. 25:31–46) The black church and black communities have historically balanced the concept of abundance with the idea of social justice. Stories are told in my family of how, during the Great Depression, no hungry stranger was turned away from the door. Today, the possibility to keep an open door policy has changed as African American societies have changed in concert with the political and economic times.

As part of an African American spirituality, longing for specifically economic justice is consistent with the overall desire for social justice. Is the current state of black America's economic condition a contradiction to the promise of abundance? Judging from the black economic conditions previously described, the answer of many black people—who struggle daily to feed, clothe, house, and educate themselves and their families—would be a resounding yes. Some black Americans may feel that black churches do not address the longing that is tied to achieving economic justice. The calls to perseverance and steadfastness that Coquet found in many black sermons might not satisfy the need to achieve social success—at a time when wonders of consumption are televised on the so-called reality programs.

Roughly 40 percent of the African American population lives in poverty. The term "fatigue" is often used to describe the state of mind of other sectors of society who have tired of particular social conditions, for instance, "diversity" fatigue or "compassion" fatigue. In a like manner, poverty fatigue would be a genuine social condition that poor people experience at a time when America—the land of so-called opportunity—is closing the doors to educational access, blaming and condemning poor people, considering all forms of social welfare ridiculous while expanding opportunities for corporate greed, expanding free market racism to new global markets, and denying that race is yet a factor in American society. Many black denominations have no satisfactory theological answer for this set of contemporary dilemmas. Some people take their problems to their church communities but are told to "pray on it." Beyond soup kitchens and food pantries, too many black churches may not offer the practical programs or resources that people need to address economic questions.

Into the midst of this social ferment come theologies of prosperity, looking like the promised land wrapped up in a winning lottery ticket to attract people who may feel they have few other options. These theologies of glitz and publicized piety capitalize on the fear and pain of people too long denied.

PROSPERITY PREACHING IN BLACK COMMUNITIES

There are different ways to think about prosperity preaching in black communities. One way is to consider particular kinds of self-identified prosperity churches. This consideration will be the focus of the next three chapters—I identify three strains of prosperity churches, each of which is powerful. This chapter looks more widely at prosperity preaching in black communities. While the first chapter weighed the historic aspects of the black church that shape black prosperity preaching today, the second chapter reflected on the concrete realities of a black spirituality of longing. Both sets of considerations influence black religious life. Both sets need to be placed in the wide frame of the black community, not reduced to one particular type of prosperity church. The connections between the past and the present, concrete realities, unsatisfied longing, and the black church became clear for me through stories.

LOOKING FOR A CHURCH HOME

The first story was told by my friend, Delores, about her and her family's search for a church home. Delores has an adult daughter who invited both Delores and Delores' mother to attend the church where she was a member. The daughter had been a member for some months and both her mother and grandmother were impressed by the positive influence the church community was having on her life. With such lived witness, both older women agreed to attend. The church had two hundred members. It was a vibrant community that seemed to be growing. Eventually both the mother and grandmother became members as well as the daughter.

But many things began to bother Delores. She was putting over one hundred dollars into her weekly collection envelope, volunteering, and attending church functions, but the pastor could never remember her name. Every event in the church cost additional fees, including Bible study. Delores became aware that the pastor could not pronounce many of the words in the Bible. At one time, he gave a sermon and challenged the community in ways that stand out in Delores' memory: "If you have to shop at KMart, you are not blessed. If you do not own your own home, you are not blessed. If you can't go out shopping whenever you want, you are not blessed. If you can't wear designer clothes, you are not blessed. And then you need to find out what sins you have committed." This idea was offensive to Delores.

Her offense at this sermon is a reminder about the importance of culture and of religious education. The pastor's words are nearly verbatim from the religious group Word of Faith, which is discussed in chapter 5. But the people who accept the teachings of those leaders have experienced a culture where the ideas are practiced and reinforced, unlike Delores' group. That pastor mistakenly thought that it is possible to start a group from that point—Do you have your designer clothes as a sign of personal salvation? A person in community must be educated, slowly, in different aspects of religious teaching. In religious education terms, this is called formation, and it is a process that begins when a person is attracted to some aspect of a religious group, whether it is the vibrancy of the service or the living witness of current members. Drawing a group together and trying to get them to swallow the religious teachings whole, without the support of a religious community that has its own culture, is not possible. Some of Delores' other experiences are evidences of the need to educate and build a religious community's faith lives.

Delores went to one of the church outings. The transportation was by car-pooled volunteers and no food was served. She realized that the amount of money charged each person was roughly four times more than the actual cost of admittance. At another time, the pastor announced that all the tithes belonged to him. Delores' breaking point came when she realized that the pastor and staff were unwilling to financially help poor people in general or the members specifically. One of the very active church members announced that she needed four hundred dollars to get home for a family funeral. The pastor said, "I've got ten dollars on it. Anybody else?"

After that, Delores went to church in anger, watching for the fall of the pastor. In a thoroughly black cultural style, Delores also helped to expose the pastor. Her actions have cultural meaning in black communities: the pastor made a black woman angry. One man expressed the impact of dealing with a black woman's anger: "If a black woman is mad at you, you might as well be dead." The situation of anger and instigation escalated over time, and Delores was willing to help it along. For instance, in one sermon, the pastor made a comment that "All the women in the church want to have sex with the pastor;" at which point, Delores said, "I burst out laughing, so hard tears were running down my face." After a few such exchanges, the pastor finally knew her name and asked if she wanted to talk to him. Her response to that invitation was cutting: "I'm not talking to Satan. I can get to hell on my own." Delores reported on the departure of the membership: "The church mothers left. Then the Christians left. There are maybe twenty-five people still there." Delores' story reveals dimensions of ways that prosperity preaching impacts black communities and ministerial realities.

What attracts most people to any church community? In Delores' case, a person who is significant to her—her daughter—invited her. The invitation was enhanced because of the positive influence the church community had on the daughter's life. Meeting a vibrant and growing church community led both Delores and her mother to join. The invitation, the positive influence, and the church community become ministerial credentials in themselves. This is an important facet of black church life: all ministers are not seminary educated. Sometimes, a person might perceive a vocational call to ministry in a particular place for a particular community. This charismatic dimension of ministry is acceptable in many black communities. Charisma is often a more important personality trait in a minister than is education. Education itself sometimes gets a bad reputation in some Christian circles, regardless of race, because it is seen as weakening the message of God through human meddling. A deacon in one church summed up the attitude: "God save me from educated Christians!"

At a time when families want to find time for each other in their busy schedules, a family membership also enhanced the attractiveness of that particular church for Delores. She may have been drawn to this church by the circumstances and connections with her family. But what other aspects draw ministers or communities to prosperity preaching?

Prosperity preachers, as will be seen in the following chapters, are models of financially successful ministers. A model wherein the minister must work a nine-to-five job to support his or her ministry habit is historic in black communities but not attractive today, especially when one or another wealthy prosperity pastor is televised several times each week. A prosperous view of ministry is certainly more tantalizing than the overworked model. In the case of Delores' ex-pastor, prosperity preaching must have seemed easy and popular enough that he tried it. But his failure with this style of preaching indicates that it is not as easy as it might appear.

For poor black people who are frustrated by their economic realities in the United States, prosperity preaching may seem a natural and obvious way to address their longings. One author contends that one of the strains of prosperity preaching that he terms "Word of Faith"

> might be seen (at least in part) as a type of "poor people's movement." The people who are its followers are primarily those whose experience has produced the desire for, if not the actualization of, upward socioeconomic mobility. This "faith formula for success" is a way of using religious doctrine to symbolically and supernaturally level the playing field with respect to access to society's resources.[1]

However, I contend that middle-class black people are also drawn to prosperity preaching, as was Delores, who is educated and not poor. There is another drawing power based on the search for a religious home. Beverly Hall Lawrence is a journalist who has noted the return of middle-class African Americans, herself included, to church participation. Her generation was the first to reap the financial benefits of the civil rights movement and the self-esteem of the "black is beautiful" consciousness era. Churches seemed in opposition to new black thinking.

My generation was one that fled churches filled with those who appeared to us to be helpless, sitting and waiting for (a white) God to intervene and settle problems for them. Many of my friends and I admit now that the idea of going to church was simply too embarrassing, because it taught people to wait for change to come and because of its reliance on European Christian symbols.[2]

While better jobs brought financial rewards, the black middle class was isolated in "a kind of limbo world—not really black or white—rather a super-black but lonely physical state of being." Security was still missing: "with the statistical failure of integration, the idea of assimilating had lost its luster for many."[3] The luster was further reduced by awareness of continued and entrenched poverty in other black sectors. Lawrence states that the need to address this was diagnosed as spiritual; church became the necessary antidote.

Nobody really wants to see going back to church as a symbol of defeat, even if we may feel personally defeated at the time. But it is in our defeated state that we seek out a place to feel comforted. It is a closing of the circle. A beacon that we finally see. A Morse code we can decipher. A common tongue. Ties that bind.[4]

Prosperity churches provide answers for black middle-class social anguish about solidifying and growing personal assets, while justifying an often new social position. These answers become enticements to participate in prosperity churches. Middle-class money is also necessary for prosperity churches to continue their own growth.

Regardless of the changes between the past and the present moments, black churches lay claim to emotional memories. The reality is that some of the churches succeed at being a comforting presence for the community while others, like the church Delores attended, do not. These images of black churches emphasize what Woodson referred to as the *socialized* church.

Yet when most black people think about church, the words of Woodson or Lincoln are not the first or fifteenth thing that comes to mind. Religion has primal emotional content for most who have been involved; that emotional content is based on cultural understandings. Identification of sacred space is part of our socialization from childhood, and so our religious memories are personal. As one example, for many African Americans sensual and strong memories of chicken dinners and hugs or preaching and praise can influence how church is viewed in the present moment. Nostalgic images of the black church include that of a bulwark against hard times, a source of inspiration and guidance, and a center for a given community.

The history of the black church ties in with current economic conditions of black Americans who carry a spirituality of longing, and these are given expression in stories like Delores'. These ideas lead to consideration of the overlapping dynamics of culture and religion in black communities that will give shape to understanding prosperity preaching and its draw for African Americans, beyond the issues of class and income. Delores was drawn to a congregation that she defined as vibrant.

In chapter 1, I stated that there are three categories of black religious life that come into sharp focus when considering prosperity preaching: shared meaning that shapes communal identity, social constructions that help shape the black community's moral values, and worship and prayer. In Delores' story, communal identity (as the pastor tried to shape meaning) and moral values (a base on which the congregation rejected the pastor) were in greater evidence. The third category requires a closer look because worship and communal prayer are critical for creating the church community that is centered on prosperity.

Most black Christian worship services include powerful preaching, culturally specific use of Scripture, and strong music ministries. African American preaching styles have moved congregations to tears or fired up community activism. Sermons are presented in a distinctive style that uses pauses and certain utterances while engaging the listeners in call-and-response dialogue. The messages of skillful black preachers are simultaneously intellectual and emotional, evoking strong responses from the listener. Martin Luther King's sermons exemplify this complexity.[5] The delivery of these messages is a form of art that is applied to political speech. The passionate declarative form has had the effect of raising the general American public's expectations of preachers and of politicians.

The Bible is used in some culturally specific ways that are only beginning to be verbalized by African American religion scholars. A collection of essays gathered by black theologian Vincent Wimbush is an example of this work that considers black cultural constructions and uses them in relation to the Bible. Wimbush asks two complex questions in the introduction to these essays that have far-reaching implications for black religious scholarship today.

> How could the formation of African America, as an example of a sociocultural formation in the West, be understood without heightened attention to the Bible, specifically, the manner in which the Bible was used as language world within which those violently cut off from their home could speak again? How could African America be explained except by reference to their decidedly political, self-defensive, and offensive use of the Bible in opposition to the uses to which white Protestants put it in the construction and confirmation of their world?[6]

Studies of African Americans and the Bible must incorporate cultural dynamics and the results will not look the same as those of white Protestants.

Music, especially gospel, is the most easily identified component of black Protestant worship services. More charismatic churches, depending on the Spirit-given gifts of members, will be more expressive and, therefore, music has an especially critical role in leading the congregation to prayer. But gospel music is also commercially popular today, becoming one of the ways that many black Americans, even if they do not regularly attend church, express and respond to life's situations. Gospel artists such as Yolanda Adams, Bebe, and Cece Winanns are so popular that their recordings are often played on black secular radio stations. The success in marketing black gospel brings other problems. Religious historian Jerma Jackson states the main benefit and problem in gospel marketing:

> As gospel gained greater exposure to the mass public, radio broadcasts and recordings made it available to audiences far removed from the black religious communities where the music had taken shape. Yet the exposure gospel gained also removed it from local control. For many who had come to regard gospel as a vital source of race pride and identity, this way of removing racial boundaries undermined black cultural autonomy and felt more intrusive than liberating.[7]

At its traditional best, black worship moves the participants to action. While this could be said of any culture's worship, there are particular aspects and expectations that are unique to black communities. Barbara Holmes, who gave definition to our understanding of the black church, also describes the power of worship that is specific to the black community. She names the meaning behind the worship experience as a contemplative practice.

> The spirit descends and the community is lifted. These practices are not unknown to researchers and church folks, but what makes these experiences also contemplative? I am suggesting that Africana worship experiences are contemplative because they create an atmosphere for communal listening and responsiveness to the manifestations of God, they impact the ethos and value system of a community, and they heal infected social and psychic wounds.[8]

Delores' story opens to discussion of some of the hidden aspects of prosperity preaching in black communities. The preaching might impact the shape of black church communities; it might become a badly delivered message, as Delores experienced. However, consideration of this preaching cannot be separated from aspects of black church life and expression. Prosperity preachers in black communities study these aspects and apply them to their congregations along with providing other answers that African Americans may feel they do not receive in other churches. Delores' story is one derived from one woman's personal experiences of church life. There are many Delores stories, but there are also many stories of satisfaction in prosperity churches. If there were not, the churches would not remain open and the church mothers and other Christians would leave. While these personal stories can be interesting, stories also happen in public view that have prosperity themes. One of these happened in Atlanta.

BLACK CHURCH, DISRUPTED AND DIVIDED

If Delores' story is that of a single woman's journey into and away from one church community, prosperity preaching has created greater, and very public, rifts in what is known as the black church. In May 2006, the seminary community of the Interdenominational

Theological Center (ITC) was divided over the invitation of Eddie Long to speak at the commencement, and the rift was publicized in the pages of the *Atlanta Journal-Constitution*. The ITC is a prominent consortium of six black seminaries, whose mission includes preparation of ministers for the black community. Some students sent a letter of protest to the president of the school questioning Long's ethics, citing his three-million-dollar income from a charity and his disdain for women and pastors of smaller churches. The three-million-dollar salary was investigated, as reported in *Black Enterprise* magazine, because its pastor

> may have violated Internal Revenue Service regulations by accepting compensation totaling $3.07 million in the use of property and salary from a charity he helped oversee. During a four-year period, he reportedly received a 20-acre, six-bedroom home estimated at $1.4 million; use of a $350,000 luxury Bentley; and more than $1 million in salary, including $494,000 in 2000. J. David Epstein, Long's tax attorney, denies any improprieties on the part of his client, insisting that the church and the charities have come to the aid of millions.[9]

In protest, several members of the board of trustees of ITC refused to participate in the graduation. Preeminent black theologian James Cone, who was to have received an honorary degree at the commencement, boycotted the ceremony when he learned of Long's engagement. The problem with Long, as reported in the *Journal-Constitution*, is that

> Long preaches what is known as prosperity gospel, that God rewards the faithful with financial success. He declared in a 2005 interview that Jesus wasn't poor. In 2003 Long told a meeting of civil rights veterans in Atlanta that blacks must "forget racism" because they had already reached the promised land. In 2004 Long led a march—while carrying a torch lit at [Martin Luther] King's crypt—where he called for a constitutional ban on gay marriage.[10]

Long, a graduate of ITC, is pastor of the largest black church in Georgia, the New Birth Missionary Baptist Church. New Birth, located on twenty-five acres and boasting a membership of more than twenty-five thousand, is a megachurch, one among many that has an impact on black religious life. The Hartford Institute for Religious Research, in a 2005 report, identifies that a megachurch has at least two thousand members. A megachurch is not necessarily a prosperity church but may be affiliated with any denomination, though the majority (56 percent) of all megachurches are evangelical.[11] While the report has some other important points, more study is needed to identify aspects of megachurches in black communities. For instance, the New Birth website includes a statement "Seven Reasons Why I Love a Big Church" that aims to dispel myths and explain the reasons and benefits for membership in a megachurch.

As I have visited many churches, I have begun to suspect that part of African Americans' attraction to large churches is the desire to be part of a successful enterprise. Large churches telegraph self-importance when a person arrives for a service: parking is acres away from the church; uniformed local law enforcement officers assist churchgoers crossing roads; and shuttles are available for the disabled. In black megachurches, the congregation becomes a self-enclosed, self-supporting community. I have wondered if re-creating a sense of a "village" in contrast to an impersonal urban world is also part of the draw. Each megachurch member with whom I have spoken has a clear sense of identity with something larger than her- or himself, even if they are at the low end of the hierarchy of the church. And the megachurches do have a clear sense of hierarchy, wherein the pastor and his or her circle are often surrounded by bodyguards and not accessible by most of the congregation. Most megachurches, and this is affirmed by the Hartford study, are structured so that members are part of smaller cells, able to relate to each other as members in this way. (One wonders: If smaller cells are needed for one to feel a sense of church, why not just be part of a smaller church?)

But the glamour provided in megachurch services, beginning with arrival at the parking lot, is part of the personal affirmation of success and security experienced by black Americans in the involvement with megachurches. In one megachurch, the elderly founding pastor died. His wake and funeral became part of the show, and so his clothes were changed every hour during the body's viewing. At the time of the actual funeral service, with an open casket, members bragged that he was in brand new suit that they had never seen. Yet this excitement has an impersonal edge: how many of the five thousand other members can one member *really* get to know? A stronger question for consideration is how has membership in black churches been changed by these distant, impersonal kinds of relationships? Does the role of the pastor become more that of a CEO, less able to minister, and ultimately more liable?

> According to John Walker, chief creative officer of Chitwood and Chitwood, a Tennessee-based accounting and financial company that represents more than 4,000 churches, many large churches now have net incomes in the hundreds of millions of dollars. Although some compare pastors of today's megachurches with Fortune 500 CEOs, pastors are not held to the same level of regulatory standards and financial accountability.[12]

Some megachurch members have spoken with me about how a pastoral service, such as a funeral, is seldom performed by the head pastor. Copastors or others are appointed for those day-to-day pastoral functions. Even leadership becomes impersonal in such a congregation.

Megachurches also emphasize the business side of religion, as maintaining the huge properties requires steady infusions of cash. Tithing has taken on new intensity. One woman told me how she had been dropped from church rolls after missing two tithing payments. This woman's story of missing tithing payments was not rejection of her Christian duty; one of her children was dying, and church members knew it. However, processes of tailoring megachurches to black communities have been adapted for prosperity churches' growth.

New Birth's vision is stated on the website, including the following:

> God's vision is to see us prosper and be in good health even as our soul prospers. . . . We believe that these are extraordinary times that call for an extraordinary people with an extraordinary anointing. . . . This is the year of ruling, subduing, and taking dominion.

. . . Nothing shall be impossible for us. God said it, we believe it, and that settles it."[13]

In contrast, ITC has a mission statement that calls for its students to "commit to and practice a liberating and transforming spirituality; academic discipline; religious, gender, and cultural diversity; and justice and peace." The ITC vision statement states that the institution "is dedicated to producing public theologians—men and women who are intellectually keen, politically sophisticated, economically savvy, culturally sensitive, family friendly, technologically literate, and spiritually astute."[14]

Rev. Long did give the commencement address at ITC and the *Atlanta Journal-Constitution* followed up the first story. During his address, Long portrayed himself as a persecuted prophet. "Long's message—like his ministry—divided the crowd anyway. While plenty of people in the chapel bolted from their seats to cheer him, others sat stoically in their seats rolling their eyes." One of the students, Victor Cyrus-Franklin, was quoted in the article: "He said at the very beginning of his message that this ceremony was about us but he spent the majority of the time talking about himself."[15]

The Long-ITC fiasco highlights how prosperity preaching is becoming a dividing factor in black church life. The anger experienced by the ministers and students from ITC seems to reflect a sense of betrayal: Long's ministry is a denial of well-developed black community and cultural identities, the very identities that the students at ITC spend years studying and learning. That Long is himself a graduate of the school is another level of betrayal for the students, because he appears to be rejecting all that they hope to achieve. Long's work denies social memories that inform black American identity. Prosperity preaching in black communities brings all these tensions into play. While Delores and her family may have rejected the clumsy attempts of one pastor who preached prosperity, would they be drawn into the web of another, especially if their hope is to find a vibrant community? Or is talk of prosperity and religion so pervasive in black communities that there is really no way to avoid it? Before moving into descriptions of three types of prosperity churches, making connections between some of the ideas from the first and second chapters will be helpful.

PROSPERITY AND BLACK RELIGION

In chapter 1, some thoughts of historical scholars about the black church shed light on our discussion of prosperity preaching. Carter Woodson defined a "conservative" strain of the black church, a strain with which prosperity churches have more in common than they do with Woodson's "progressive" churches. E. Franklin Frazier talked about business as a way to insure social acceptance of black Americans; in like manner, prosperity preaching offers a corporatized model that promotes financial success as a component of Christianity. C. Eric Lincoln called for a black church with a "mature religious posture." Perhaps today's prosperity churches will claim they have reached that place.

Most significantly, today's prosperity preachers reach out to provide answers to the black community's spirituality of longing, suggesting that emptiness can be filled with steady incoming cash flows. The Urban League's 2005 equality index lays out the dimensions of socially constructed black economic woes. Tavis Smiley's *Covenant with Black America* encourages discussion in order to actively address social inequalities. But religions that emphasize prosperity as realized spirituality move the discussions from the intellectual to the emotional realm. They direct black folks' attention toward a superficial materialism, as does Reginald Lewis' title "*Why Should White Guys Have All the Fun?*" The unquestioning approach of prosperity preaching implies that patriarchal imperialism is "fun," not admitting its good times are restricted to only very few. With this focus, prosperity churches trump wider concerns for social justice with an extended meditation on acquired money and goods as a spiritual right. This focus is reminiscent of a 1903 warning from W. E. B. Du Bois: "What if the Negro people be wooed from a strife for righteousness, from a love of knowing, to regard dollars as the be-all and end-all of life?"[16] Du Bois warned that there is more to life than money; prosperity preaching may bring more of the "black nihilism" of which Cornel West warned. He defines nihilism as "the lived experience of coping with a life of horrifying meaninglessness, hopelessness, and (most important) lovelessness. The frightening result is a numbing detachment from others and a self-destructive disposition toward the world."[17]

I imagine that a challenge would come from those who are involved in prosperity religions. Clearly these theologies give hope to African Americans, building self-esteem and a deeper sense of American citizenship, in ways that many black churches have not been able to in recent times. Is that such a bad thing? The theologies that drive these churches of prosperity do indeed give folks fast access to a sense of personal power and self-esteem. The lessons taught in these churches imbue the listeners with hope. But is this really hope? I heard the story of a pastor in a well-established black prosperity church who has heads of big game from various spots in the world that he has hunted and killed hanging on the wall of his office. Is knowing that the pastor draws enough salary (from tithes) that he can trek the globe and kill animals a sign of black progress? Is this economic progress? If so, what is the measure of that progress? Animal trophies as indicator of black economic achievement cannot be found in Scripture, in the Urban League's documents, or in the *Covenant with Black America*. Du Bois' question holds up the traditional African American striving for justice combined with a desire for education as values that should be held dearly. How does prosperity preaching work toward the greater good while standing on the shoulders of those who came before and sacrificed for our benefit today?

But Du Bois is not as well publicized today as are prosperity preachers and their ideas. Prosperity ideas are reported in black media sources other than the recordings, books, frequently televised programs, and well-developed websites of different churches that will be discussed in chapters 5 and 6. *Essence* magazine published an article on one prosperity church: "A Dollar and A Dream: Pastors Creflo and Taffi Dollar have built a multimillion-dollar megachurch empire by practicing what they preach."[18]

Prosperity theology ideas are so pervasive today that black communities are influenced, consciously or not. For instance, the language of "blessing" has become so common as to be almost meaningless among African Americans. The greeting, "Have a nice day," has been supplanted by the phrase "Have a blessed day." A person may respond to the question "How are you?" with "I'm blessed." These kinds of statements are common among young black people;

rappers outfitted in tight clothing and dripping with gold accessories are quick to talk in terms of blessings. Blessing is a concept that ignores a person's talents or effort, and personal achievement is downplayed with a false humility.

The rise of new prosperity churches in the last fourth of the twentieth century did not raise warning flags among existing black churches. Their existence was just one more form of black religious creativity. But as these prosperity churches have extended their influence in black communities, they can no longer be dismissed. Prosperity churches signal changes in black religious life, ministry, and the meaning of "the" black church. They intersect with political and social life in new ways, creating new and often uncomfortable meanings that counter the status quo that exists in black communities. Most importantly, these churches are changing the constructions of black theology. These ideas will be explored in more detail in the last two chapters, after looking at three expressions of formalized prosperity preaching, beginning with the ways that theologies of prosperity historically were shaped in African American Christian religious life.

4 | OLD SCHOOL PROSPERITY PREACHING

The stresses from economic deprivation, lack of control, and domination by others are not new in black communities. Nor are religious responses that can be termed "prosperity preaching." Yet there are significant differences between the past and the present in the ways that churches answered the longing of black Americans for economic justice. Religious responses prior to the 1970s were, in most cases, shaped by the realities of legal segregation; black participation in the American economy was even more restricted than it is now.

DEVELOPING (NEW) IDEAS

The twentieth century was the first one that black Americans could begin as a struggling but not enslaved people. Black intellectuals developed many ideas about what should be done to insure and advance the limited freedoms they had. They were also able to soak up the intellectual and spiritual life of the country, as they had not been able to before. Many new religious movements influenced the American public, including African Americans. Historian Jill Watts describes the influence these had in the development of Father Divine's religious ideas. In the 1840s, inventor Phineas Quimby began the New Thought movement, which involved the use of the mind to cure the body. Mary Baker Eddy, one of Quimby's students, added a spiritual component and began the Christian Science organization, believing that "tuning into God's inner-dwelling presence and achieving oneness with his spirit restored health and well being."[1] Quimby also influenced Myrtle and Charles Fillmore in their development of the Unity School in early 1900. Watts argues that, for these thinkers,

The mind was a powerful instrument that shaped human destiny. While sin, sickness, and misfortune resulted from negative thinking, awareness of God's internal presence and the power of positive thought allowed men and women to overcome adversity and actualize their desires. But Fillmore . . . [contended] that positive thinking brought mortals close to divinity.[2]

The Fillmores' thinking is particularly important for the development of the ministry of Johnnie Colemon, which is discussed in chapter 6.

Another aspect of the development of prosperity theologies occurred during the nineteenth century as Americans, particularly in the Northeast, experimented with other aspects of the mind-and-body connection and shaped other religious trends of their time, including Transcendentalism, Mesmerism, and Spiritualism. In 1927 Ernest Holmes combined Quimby's ideas of healing with the Fillmores' and other mystical trends of the time and founded Science of Mind or Religious Science, focusing on the spiritual aspects of mental control.[3] As black Americans migrated from the South, they would have encountered these religious ideas but were not members of the religious movements. While many scholars posit that black Americans found these new religious concepts and adopted them, I take a different view as a result of my research and interviews. With some black people who have been members of these churches, I propose that such transfer of ideas did not happen so simply. Black Americans retained concepts about religion that have African roots. These concepts became part of black creative religious responses to encountering Christianity, shaping other forms of faith expression that extend across the African diaspora: Voudou, Candomble, Lukumì, Obeah, and so on. A quote by Zora Neale Hurston from her 1930s research on the religious life of Southern black Americans underlines this idea:

> The Negro has not been christianized as extensively as is generally believed. The great masses are still standing before their pagan altars and calling old gods by a new name. As evidence of this, note the drum-like rhythm of all Negro spirituals. All Negro-made church music is dance-possible.[4]

Black Americans probably did encounter these ideas because of the changes in publishing religious writers. One historian, Matthew Hedstrom, traced the early twentieth century emergence of the religious middlebrow through published works. Middlebrow is a term adopted by some scholars

> to describe the new cultural forms that emerged when "high culture" was marketed to a growing, socially anxious American middle class seeking to "better" itself in the decades following World War I. . . . Freer than ever to browse widely in the marketplace of ideas, millions of Americans in the 1920s, '30s, and '40s discovered mysticism.[5]

Publishing religious ideas became an aspect that shaped American religious culture, the beginning of a media explosion that is critically important in the growth of the prosperity theologies discussed in the following two chapters.

To imply, however, that black people's accidental exposure to books on New Thought, Unity, or Mesmerism was the sole reason for the religious development resulting in Daddy Grace or Father Divine denies the existence of an African-derived faith consciousness. Perhaps the New Thought ideas resonated with and affirmed the concepts that black people already held about the power of the Divine's abilities to manifest in and through daily life. This is a continuing controversy, especially as the Unity/Science of Mind aspects of prosperity theology took on new meaning in the late twentieth century (as will be discussed in chapter 6).

By the 1930s, the Great Depression had taken a firm hold on the nation. Black Americans were mostly already on the lower end of the economic spectrum, and the Depression only made their conditions worse. Black people fought in and were affected by the First and Second World Wars, which took them to new countries and brought new experiences. Throughout this time, economic troubles continued in the still segregated black communities. By the end of the 1960s, other changes began as a result of the civil rights movement, but the spirituality of longing continued.

To try to find a remedy for economic troubles in churches—specifically those institutions that were operated by African

Americans in ways that responded to black cultures—was a logical move. But there was more involved. Some black preachers and ministers in the twentieth century found ways to creatively shape their theologies. This chapter describes two different uses of religion with prosperity themes.

SWEET DADDY GRACE AND FATHER DIVINE

The figure of the flamboyant black preacher is well known and often caricatured today. But in the early part of the twentieth century, the need for new visions through churches was genuine and pressing. As African American religious historian Gayraud Wilmore states,

> The economic and psychological pressures of the Depression and the brutality of racism drove blacks deeper into themselves for a spiritual reserve with which to survive. . . . During the 1920s and 1930s most black churches retained a basically rural orientation and retreated into enclaves of moralistic, revivalistic Christianity, by which they tried to fend off the encroaching gloom and pathology of the ghetto. As far as challenging white society, or seeking to mobilize the community against poverty and oppression, most churches were too otherworldly, apathetic, or caught up in institutional maintenance to deal with such issues.[6]

While Wilmore's statement may seem to critical to some, his statement hits on black Americans' need for something religiously different and more fulfilling, especially those folks traveling from the South to urban settings in the North during the Great Migrations. Daddy Grace and Father Divine offered alternatives.

In 1881, Marcelino Manoel de Graca was born in the Cape Verde Islands. He moved to New Bedford, Massachusetts, in 1903, changed his name to Charles Manuel Grace, and established his first House of Prayer in 1919. In the May 2006 Pictorial Revue published by the United House of Prayer, this beginning is described:

> Through the Supreme Sacrifice of our beloved Founder, Sweet Daddy Grace, the United House of Prayer was established in America in the early 1900's. He built the very first House of Prayer structure in West Wareham MA in the year 1919, with his own hands [symbolizing "a grain of a mustard seed"]. From this

humble beginning, hundreds of Houses of Prayer spread across America, as this faith went on to become one of the largest single denominations in America.[7]

Daddy Grace brought excitement and the possibilities of fulfilling dreams to his followers. He cultivated a glamorous image, calling himself the "boyfriend of the world":

> With his long flowing hair, two-inch fingernails (painted red, white, and blue), cutaway coat, and chauffeured limousines, the bishop struck an impressive if not awesome figure. . . . He would admonish his followers . . . "Never mind about God. Salvation is by Grace . . . Grace has given God a vacation, and since God is on His vacation, don't worry him. . . . If you sin against God, Grace can save you, but if you sin against Grace, God cannot save you."[8]

Prosperity was preached by Grace as "he promised his followers spiritual as well as material rewards that they could have in the present."[9] He symbolized that prosperity in his lavish lifestyle—surrounded by homes and cars. His approach to expanding his churches was pragmatic, completely paying for a building before it was dedicated as a House of Prayer. "Those members of the congregation who may not own their own homes can point with pride to their partial ownership in the Houses of Prayer."[10]

The members do indeed own the properties, as this author states:

> These are a few extracts taken from the "General Council Laws of the United House of Prayer for all People" that illustrate the emphasis on money: Pastors must be in knowledge of everything: every penny raised and spent. All pastors must see to it that each member pays his convocation fee and substantial rallies put on for the upbuilding of the Kingdom of Heaven and this is to be put in the hands of our General Builder to build as he see fit without bounds. All Houses of Prayer must raise money in a united drive to buy a car for our Daddy Grace. Each state must do its part.[11]

The sexism inherent in the religion constructed by the "boyfriend of the world" continues to the present: women are not expected to lead the community. "Although women in most of the Houses outnumber men two or three to one, they are forbidden (based on Scripture) from advancing in the church's hierarchy to positions of minister or elder."[12] The connections between sexism, patriarchy (as exemplified by the title "Daddy," continued by Grace's successors "Daddy" McCullough and "Daddy" Madison), and prosperity will be discussed in the final two chapters.

Father Divine's childhood history, even his real name, is recounted differently. In one version, he began life as George Baker Jr., born May 1879 in Maryland. In this version, he grew up in a cabin with fourteen others, the adults eking out a living on subsistence wages. George lived with hand-me-downs and a poor diet.[13] In other versions told by Divine, he was either born in 1877 or 1883 in Georgia or Virginia or other southern states. It only added to the confusion when, in 1936, a woman named Elizabeth said that Divine was her son, originally named Frederick Edwards and born in North Carolina.[14]

Regardless of this blurred history (adding to his mystique as a messianic figure), he fully experienced the impact on the black community of undereducation and underemployment. His religious views reflected these social conditions. During a time in Baltimore, when he still understood himself as the "Messenger" of God, he stated: "God is not only personified and materialized. He is repersonified and rematerialized. He rematerializes and he rematerialates. He repersonificates and He repersonifitizes."[15] He saw beggars in Baltimore and saw this as a blasphemy against God. "They were trying to sell the body of God in my consideration—even the spirit thereof." The beggars' experiences also caused him to reflect on the processes of fundraising in churches. "It was not according to the life and teachings of the Christ. Therefore, I said within myself, 'I will go forth and prove to the people that the Gospel can be preached without money and without price!'"[16] He continued his evangelizing travels, preaching a new order while developing his theology.

In 1914, after a period of incarceration, he went to Valdosta, Georgia. He preached at a black Holiness Church that "God's second appearance on earth was in the form of a Jew and that now he comes in the form of a Negro. He told them he was going to bring the world to an end before long."[17] While the congregation threw the Messenger out, there were several black women in Valdosta attracted to the message, which "reinforced their religious convictions and liberated them from oppressive roles." The Messenger rejected gender roles and promoted celibacy among his followers. "Radicalized, his female disciples began to rebel against their traditional roles. After worshiping with him, one woman returned home and began beating her husband." The town had had enough. The chief of police arrested him, putting him on trial for lunacy. His followers in town, some of whom were white, continued to agitate outside the jail and in the courtroom. When on the stand, the Messenger was ordered to prove his divinity, "He explained that he did not produce miracles, but they were generated 'by the spirit that works in him.' He insisted that faith fueled miracles and, since the courtroom observers lacked faith, such phenomena were impossible." He was found guilty of insanity by a jury, but was not institutionalized.[18]

In 1917, he moved to New York City, changing his name to Reverend St. John Divine, or Father Divine. He opened Peace Missions in Harlem and New Jersey. He opened another mission in Los Angeles in 1937. The services were joyful experiences, "Heaven on earth," and this was especially true of the "Kingdom banquet." In a 1938 account from the Federal Writers' Project, Frank Byrd wrote of his experience at one of the banquets.

> About nine o'clock in the evening the official feasting begins. Gathered about the Father are his legal satellites, staff members, personal attendants, followers, and sympathizers. The table is modeled somewhat after the accepted seating arrangement of Christ and his disciples at the Last Supper, with the exception of the fact that where Christ seated twelve Father Divine seats hundreds. Interested outsiders are segregated to side tables. . . . The table is heavily loaded with fresh fruits of every description, whole hams, chickens, suckling pigs, legs of lamb, pig's [sic] knuckles, pork chops, baked breast of lamb, beef-stew, corn, cabbage, kale, spinach, potatoes, rice, celery, sliced tomatoes, large bowls of chopped lettuce and green peppers, cakes, pies, pitchers of coffee and milk. . . . When the meal is well under way, Father Divine rises, beams (as only Father Divine can beam) and says in that crisp, energetic way: "Peace, everyone! Righteousness, Justice and

Truth, Good Health, with Good Manners and Good Behavior for you! By so doing and so being, we will have a righteous government in which to live. Is everybody happy?"[19]

In this excerpt, the images of prosperity were made concrete to the participants, many still suffering from the economic realities of the Depression, with a banquet. But Divine's idea of prosperity needs clarification. It was not ever a handout needed by the poor, which was degrading and only resulted in subsistence living. Instead he promoted the development of businesses and thereby autonomy.

> By the mid-1930s the Peace Mission had become the largest realty holder in Harlem, with three apartment houses, nine private houses, fifteen to twenty flats, and several meeting halls with dormitories on the upper floors. In addition, followers in Harlem operated some twenty-five restaurants, six groceries, ten barber shops, ten cleaning stores, two dozen huckster wagons with clams and oysters or fresh vegetables, and a coal business with three trucks ranging from Harlem to the mines in Pennsylvania.[20]

Because members lived in communal settings in "Peace Mission Evangelical hotels," lived frugally, and put the proceeds back into the common pool, these businesses could thrive during a time when other businesses were failing.

Father Divine and Daddy Grace each had a presence and impact on the religious consciousness of black communities. The statement that a preacher is like one or the other of these men can still be heard in black communities, often as derogatory statements. While both men built thriving and glamorous ministries with some emphasis on money, many African Americans found their well-publicized and often ridiculed antics—from court cases to money troubles to theological statements—flat out embarrassing. If a spirituality of longing filled African Americans with desire for financial fulfillment, it also filled them with a longing for social acceptance as well. Many have been very conscious of doses of bad press and poor public opinions that build on stereotypes of black people. Therefore negative media portrayals of stupid, uneducated, or criminal black people rankle. An example highlights this contention.

Father Divine and Daddy Grace were sometimes considered rivals. Therefore, in 1938, *Time* magazine reported on the move of Grace to Harlem, through his purchase of one of Divine's buildings.

Rev. Major J. ("Father") Divine, Harlem cultist whose followers believe he is God, has many "extensions" or "kingdoms." Chief one until last week was a three-story building, rank with human and culinary odors, which he rented on Manhattan's 115th Street. Why this kingdom had not long since collapsed was the wonder of any outsider who ever attended a meeting there, felt its floor reverberate to the rhythmic pounding of a thousand Corybantic Negro feet. Many a Harlemite believes the black "God's" following is dwindling. Last week Father Divine's chief kingdom, still apparently in good shape, was sold to a black rival—"Bishop" Charles Manuel ("Daddy") Grace. Assessed at $38,000 and owned by a Manhattan bank, the kingdom was first offered to the Divineites but their agent, named "Blessed Purin Heart," balked at paying more than $16,000. Bishop Grace paid down $2,000 in cash. . . . Grace calls his sect the "House of Prayer for All People." . . . In his 100 churches, pastors exhort the faithful for contributions, and during services . . . there are likely to be frequent sales talks and demonstrations of Daddy Grace Toothpaste, Daddy Grace Cold Cream, Daddy Grace Hair Straightener. Pastors also hawk the *Grace Magazine*, a "miraculous publication" over which prayers are said as it goes through the presses.[21]

The article continued in this derogatory tone, including a brief listing of both men's financial and legal troubles. In 1938, a press release in a nationally distributed magazine that showed black people in a ridiculous light would not have been welcomed in black communities. The article would have further reinforced the racist beliefs of the majority of Americans. Black people battle such negative stereotyping, often calling for black unity. This communal protective mindset leads to other expressions of black loyalty. So while some black ministers' public accounts opposing the divinity claims of Divine or Grace may be found in court records, the depth of communal antipathy against either man may only be gauged by negative views of both that continue to be voiced quietly in black communities.

GARVEY AND FORMAN

Two other expressions of prosperity thinking and preaching from the twentieth century have most often been researched from the perspective of black socialist movements. This may have some validity, but that approach cannot explain the relationships with religious thought, often glossed over by the researcher. Also, the majority of black Americans might be hard pressed to identify their spirituality of longing with socialism. One set of ideas began around the time of Divine and Grace, through the organizational development of Marcus Garvey (1887–1940) and the establishment and continuation of the Pan African Orthodox Church. The other prosperity-related religious idea came later in the century, in 1969, resonating with efforts for civil rights or black power; a direct economic challenge to white churches was literally thrown down by James Forman and the Black Manifesto. Both these efforts were countercultural, carving new responses to black economic realities using creative religious perspectives.

Garvey's response was the construction of a political and organizational effort to return to Africa. An activist of the Harlem Renaissance, Garvey was a Jamaican who founded the United Negro Universal Improvement Association (UNIA), which looked to build self-sufficient, independent black communities. With little success in Jamaica, he traveled to Harlem in 1916, where his organization flourished for a number of years before Garvey was deported in 1927 for embezzlement. His vision encompassed the return of all willing black people to African shores. He saw black people sharing a common bond that transcended whatever nation they lived in. Garvey's idea was not simply justice for oppressed black people, but for all to come together in a new African empire.

> Everybody knows that there is absolutely no difference between the native African and the American and West Indian Negroes, in that we are descendants from one common family stock. It is only a matter of accident that we have been divided and kept apart for over three hundred years, but it is felt that when the time has come for us to get back together, we shall do so in the spirit of brotherly love. . . . We desire to help them build up *Africa as a Negro Empire*, where every black man, whether he was born in

Africa or in the Western world, will have the opportunity to develop on his own lines under the protection of the most favorable democratic institutions.[22]

To do this, Garvey advocated black self-sufficiency, developing all aspects of a total black society, "political, religious, social, recreational, cultural, and economic," black religious historian Gayraud Wilmore delineates. Wilmore cites the preamble to the UNIA's constitution:

> The Universal Negro Improvement Association and African Communities League is a social, friendly, humanitarian, charitable, educational, institutional, constructive, and expansive society, and is founded by persons, desiring to the utmost to work for the general uplift of the Negro peoples of the world. . . . The motto of the organization is: One God! One Aim! One Destiny! Therefore, let justice be done to all mankind.[23]

Historian Randall Burkett has analyzed the religious ethos of the UNIA and found that there were religious themes throughout the structure of the organization. Scripture, for instance, was used to prove that the UNIA was to establish an African nation, as taught in the *Universal Negro Catechism*:

> Q. What prediction made in the 68th Psalm and the 31st verse is now being fulfilled"
>
> A. "Princes shall come out of Egypt, Ethiopia shall soon stretch forth her hands unto God."
>
> Q. What does this verse prove?
>
> A. That Negroes will set up their own government in Africa, with rulers of their own race.[24]

Garvey's organization constructed a total view of reality, one that was specifically grounded in black culture and one that rejected oppressive white European culture. He established the African Orthodox Church and encouraged black people to envision a black God, as all humans are made in that image. It was decided at the 1924 annual UNIA convention, because Muslims and other non-Christians were Garveyites, that Christianity was not the organization's official religion. The idea of a black Madonna and Child was also promoted at that same convention.[25]

The influence of Garvey's value-laden religious views has continued. The Pan African Orthodox Church, or the Shrine of the Black Madonna, considers itself the inheritor of the Garvey tradition. The Shrine began in the late 1960s in Detroit under the direction of Albert Cleage. The values of black self-determination and community building grounded in religion, counter to (white) American consumerism is reflected in one black educator's reflection on education. Shelley McIntosh has been a member of the Pan African Orthodox Church for over thirty years. She is a cardinal in the religion and, as an educator, has worked with the Children's Community, or Mtoto House. The Children's Community was developed and based on a "theological framework that emphasizes the concept of nation as sacred; a commitment to end oppression; group processes that facilitate an individual's movement from being self-centered to group-centered; and rituals and practices that erode the walls of alienation."[26] The cardinal's values are reflected as she views black children outside her community.

> I see a fourteen-year-old female sitting on her young boyfriend's lap at a Coney Island while her younger sister, who looks about twelve-years old, observes this. The younger one talks and acts in a fast, sassy way. She too is flirting with her sister's boyfriend. "Let me call my daddy on your cell phone," she asks her sister's boyfriend. "Hi, daddy. Are you still wearing that same hairstyle? I need $100." The boyfriend chimes in. "Tell him to send me $50." I wanted to say, "Little girl, get off of his lap and let me talk to all three of you about some goals in your lives." Instead I look and when I leave I offer a friendly smile. My heart goes out to all these children and I feel that in today's world, many need a total institution that could save their lives.[27]

The presence of such values that counter the economic values experienced by the majority of African Americans will be something to remember when considering the preaching of some prosperity pastors today. Delores' pastor and Eddie Long, mentioned in the first chapter, would find this woman's ideas laughable. McIntosh's words are reminders that black communities are not and never have been monolithic in their views and values.

The story of James Forman and the Black Manifesto also begins in Detroit in the 1960s. If Depression era African Americans were under stress from their economic conditions, the hope that civil rights would make great change in black lives was challenged by black power ideas from such thinkers as Angela Davis and Malcolm X. Calling for deeper social change and emphasizing human rights caused some African Americans to rethink what black Americans really needed. In Detroit in April 1969, the delegates to the Black Economic Development Conference considered different ways to economically strengthen and develop black communities. James Forman, an activist leader in the Student Non-Violent Coordinating Committee, penned the "Black Manifesto to the White Christian Churches and the Jewish Synagogues in the United States of America and All Other Racist Institutions." Agreed to by the conference participants, the Manifesto demanded five hundred million from white Christian churches and Jewish synagogues. The total was determined at the rate of fifteen dollars for each black American.

> We know that the churches and synagogues have a tremendous wealth, and its membership—white America—has profited and still exploits black people. We are also not unaware that the exploitation of colored people around the world is aided and abetted by the white Christian churches and synagogues. . . . Underneath all this exploitation, the racism of this country has produced a psychological effect upon us that we are beginning to shake off. We are no longer afraid to demand our full rights as a people in this decadent society.[28]

The plan was to use the money for very concrete economic development in black communities, including to establish a bank, establish publishing houses and television stations, set up a National Black Labor Strike and Defense fund, and establish a Black Anti-Defamation League. Here was a new way to think about prosperity and religion.

The Manifesto was not mailed to various churches but dramatically presented beginning May 4, 1969. Gayraud Wilmore describes the scene:

It was the dramatic appearance of James Forman at Riverside Church, bearded and brandishing his staff like an Old Testament prophet, that galvanized the attention of the nation and brought a storm of outrage from white clergy and laity. The bold disruption of the services at Riverside Church, one of the most prestigious congregations in the country, alienated many liberal whites from the aggressive policies advocated by [the National Committee for Black Church Men].[29]

In this view, prosperity was defined from a humanist perspective, related to economic justice. Religion, in particular organized religion, was seen as opportunity to achieve some significant social restructuring in black communities. It is clear from the perspective of the twenty-first century that the challenge was thrown to churches and synagogues, first because so many church people had participated in the civil rights movements, declaring their anger at racism. But more than this made churches and synagogues important partners in working for justice: if the claims of Christianity were to be believed, and the sufferings of Jewish people who had been through their own holocaust had any meaning, it would be a natural presupposition that they would welcome the occasion to make significant changes to America's inequitable social structures.

Forman's dramatic call to action achieved limited results. In 1970, one author bitterly stated:

Thus far, judging by their response to the Black Manifesto, the churches have failed. . . . Church bureaucrats and churchmen have not understood that ways must be found to connect the leadership of discontented colored and white millions to a broad-based and coordinated political process aimed at empowering the alienated urban poor and lower middle class. . . . The overall response of churches and synagogues to the Black Manifesto, and especially to Forman's language and tactics, betrayed considerable ignorance of the dimensions of our domestic crisis.[30]

Both Garvey with the UNIA and Forman with the Black Manifesto struggled for new definitions of prosperity, linking those definitions firmly to actualized justice. Both demonstrated that there are a range of possible responses when addressing African

Americans and economic disparities. Both Garvey and Forman questioned the values born of our struggles and whether the experiences of being black in America yields any other information than assimilation.

THE SHAPE OF PROSPERITY PREACHERS

These four expressions of prosperity preaching from the twentieth century, before the current crop of such preachers, share several features. They each draw concepts from cultural perspectives and then direct the results back to black communities, sometimes for active change. Daddy Grace brought a glamorous image; Father Divine enticed members with a heavenly feast and a business sense. Marcus Garvey brought a new social vision; James Forman tried to bring about new relationships between race, economic justice, and religion. One author's term, "folk cultural associations," applies to these constructions of prosperity and religion.

> The hallmark of the folk cultural associations is that they are indigenous and autonomous groups, free to create their own social world. They are spontaneously generated by their members rather than consciously shaped and directed by an outside force. In their self-reliance, they draw on culturally derived innovations and an aesthetic fluidity based on African American folk cultural traditions. Moreover, the folk cultural equation and, to an extent, also the popular, ensures the persistence of African-based cultural adaptations.[31]

These early black folk cultural responses to poverty and prosperity in America were conscious of social ills and culturally responsive in their resulting conceptualization. Each response was aware of the importance of creating a culturally relevant spectacle, or in Forman's case, the grand gesture, that would resonate with their communities. Despite the creativeness of their ideas, each resultant group was overly dependent on charismatic leadership to bring the plans to fruition.

But changes have occurred in American social structures since the Black Manifesto. The liberal retreat from race, poor education, free market racism, and continued marginalization of great numbers of black Americans has continued. The new theologies of prosperity in the United States have responded to these changes even as they have altered the focus, and by extension, black religious life. As these churches and theologies are considered in the next two chapters, questions this chapter has raised will return. Does prosperity mean being like "them"? Or is it possible to be "us"? Can black Americans afford to dream new dreams through enriched faith lives that will redress *longing*?

5 | THE HAGIN/COPELAND SCHOOL OF PROSPERITY

O ne of the most visible of today's black prosperity preachers is Creflo Dollar (Georgia). He is not alone in his approach, which is called Word of Faith. Other black
preachers from the same line who will be discussed in
this chapter are Leroy Thompson (Louisiana), and, with a curious
twist, Fred Price (California). These stories, though, begin outside
the black community, with a white preacher, Kenneth Hagin, as he
developed his theology beginning in 1934 in Texas. The prosperity
gospel went into overdrive about thirty years later with the efforts of
Kenneth Copeland, also in Texas, who successfully propagated the
message through various media with a vengeance.

HAGIN AND COPELAND: Shaping Prosperity Theologies

Kenneth Hagin Sr., who was white, is often considered the founding father of the Word of Faith movement. His work was founda-
tional for the development of current theologies of prosperity. He
was from a poor background, and the beginning of his ministry was
seen as his own miraculous healing from "a deformed heart and in-
curable blood disease at the age of 17."[1] Over the years he expanded
the ministry through evangelistic crusades around the country, publishing a magazine, and establishing various Bible schools and ministerial alliance groups.

But some have questioned Hagin's originality in the ideas of
Word of Faith. Some have pointed to a lesser-known thinker who
died in 1948, E. W. Kenyon, as the originator of the concepts. There
are some similarities between Kenyon and Hagin, as one author
points out. Both were poor and

had limited formal education and distrusted denominational creeds and structures—particularly academically trained theologians. Both men had switched their denominational affiliations at least once in their lives, eventually becoming independent. They founded Bible training centers to pass on their teachings to new generations of church leaders, and used the mass media—radio in particular—to further their message. At the heart of the message was their promotion of a higher, "better" life that faithful Christians can experience if only they are taught to alter their thinking and be bold enough to expect more than mere spiritual blessing.[2]

Regardless of these similarities, it was Hagin who was most influential in establishing a line of prosperity preachers. The Bible schools and ministerial alliances, in particular, have helped provide a foundation and support network for various prosperity ministers, who meet and work together at conferences, especially the annual Rhema conference. Hagin's son continues his ministries today, and this will be important in the Fred Price story told later in this chapter.

Milmon Harrison is a former member of one of the churches who outlines the three main beliefs of the movement. The first is knowing that Christians who truly believe have been promised abundant life in the contractual agreement of the Bible that is "available to anyone who dares to trust in the promises of God . . . and will simply *name* what they want and then *claim* it as theirs by faith."[3] Those Christians who live with physical or emotional suffering, or even under the "curse" of poverty, are those who are not fully living their faith potential. These biblical promises of abundance are actually spiritual laws that can be applied by anyone. "People who have degrees—especially if they disagree with the movement's teachings—are frequently depicted in its literature and by its ministers as having allowed their education to hinder their ability to read the Bible and to understand what God 'really' means to say."[4]

Second, the members hold to positive confession, again stressing, "name it and claim it." Each person must speak positively of the coming blessing, to be fulfilled as God certainly promised. If the person in any way doubts, it will stop the blessing from flowing to them. Third, "contemporary notions of designer clothes and other conspicuous symbols of material success are turned back and used as a lens through which to understand and redefine God's promises to give the believer a life of abundance."[5] These three ideas become the driving force and focal points of these Word of Faith style theologies. They will come up again and again in different forms. To retain the centrality of these concepts, both Scripture and the significance of day-to-day events must be constantly refined to fit the framework.

Kenneth Copeland excels at this. Under his leadership, theologies of prosperity have flourished in new ways. His managerial expertise has helped him to create a well-financed model of ministry, stepping into a slicker, more commercially viable model of prosperity. If Hagin was the seed, Copeland became the flower. The expansion of his ministry was aided greatly by the Trinity Broadcast Network, which began in 1973 (also in Texas). This network has been a significant location for bringing all manner of evangelical Christian programming to the United States as well as other countries. With the use of television, the "look" and style of a preacher became an important way that Americans judged the sincerity and honesty of their preachers. Copeland, for instance, uses his wife as a more visible prop for advertising. For example, his books and website will show at least one picture of him with his wife, in a pose emulating a *Father Knows Best/Leave it to Beaver* 1950s sincerity. Copeland has expanded his ministry to Australia, South Africa, Britain, and Canada. This international expansion brings a new dimension to prosperity ideas.

> What is the gospel to the poor? *The gospel to the poor is that Jesus has come and they don't have to be poor anymore!* . . . [Some missionaries] will argue "You can preach abundance in the United States, but don't come to Africa and preach it." Or, they tell me, "It won't work in El Salvador." "It won't work in Nicaragua," etc. *But when you are preaching the Word of God, it works.* . . . There is enough undiscovered wealth in the poorest nations of this world to turn their poverty into abundance if they would just believe the gospel.[6]

In a strange video clip on the website YouTube, Kenneth Hagin and Kenneth Copeland are seen together, most likely at a conference of such preachers. The clip is subtitled "Pentecostal Bedlam." It shows

Hagin leading the participants in a bout of laughing, staggering around, at times held up by several men, giggling and muttering "drunk ag'in." This is most likely a reflection on a line from Acts of the Apostles when the Holy Spirit came on the disciples after Christ's ascension. In the scripture story, as the disciples began speaking in tongues and all understood, the bystanders who witnessed the event were baffled and asked if those disciples had had too much wine, were they drunk? (Acts 2:13) What is seen on the video clip is a kind of mass hysteria, as participants are shown enacting drunken behavior for about six minutes. In the front row of the crowd, with some rolling on the floor, are Kenneth Copeland and his wife.[7] (One of the lone black faces in this same crowd appeared to be Leroy Thompson, whose ministry will be discussed in the next section.) The six minutes of this video did not bring a sense of religious quest or spiritual peace. Instead I kept thinking that these ministers were celebrating all the way to the bank, and the joke was not really funny.

The Word of Faith group of churches and ministers should be considered a distinctive religious denomination, having not only its own creed and set of beliefs, but leadership that assists in establishing satellite churches through Rhema and various ministry education centers.

These Word of Faith theologies of prosperity are firmly wedded to a view of America's world dominance and to capitalism that is exclusively, unapologetically patriarchal. All of this is explained as God's will. The patriarchal idea is important, becoming an integral part of the picture of God-directed life the Word of Faith preachers paint. It also assists the church founder to set up a religious dynasty, one that is passed from father to son, as Hagin Sr. passed his church and center to Hagin Jr. Women are part of the dynasty, providing directions for women members' lives. Acceptable members of the family are able to obtain education (relevant to their idea of church-building) and then jobs through the church. The nuclear family of the pastor is involved—and revered—by the members of the church. One overall objective of this denomination seems to be that a given church will be nurtured in such a way as to grow into a megachurch. The impersonality of megachurches, evidenced by the distance of people from leadership, seems to add to the programmed mystique of the leadership and the evidence of "prosperity," which the people can attain by default by just attending the church.

None of these ideas were questioned as African American male preachers adopted this thinking. The new prosperity-by-Word-of-Faith versions of black preachers are different from Daddy Grace or Father Divine. The latter two had established links, however tenuous, between prosperity and healing and justice for black people. Black Word of Faith prosperity preachers set themselves up as those leading other African Americans from oppression, but they are so different from Garvey or Forman that no comparison is sensible.

LEROY THOMPSON

Leroy Thompson's church is the Word of Life Christian Center, also the center of the Ever Increasing Word Ministries, located in Darrow, Louisiana. The Dollar work is better known, but I begin here because several things became clear for me about Word of Faith and its presence in black communities. The Ever Increasing church is smaller than Dollar's, claiming seventeen hundred members. But Thompson is older and had been pastoring at the same church—known then as Mount Zion Baptist—for a number of years. He writes that he received Bachelor's, Master's, Doctorate of Theology, and Doctorate of Divinity degrees from the Christian Bible College of Louisiana and identifies himself as Doctor Thompson. When Thompson became involved in Hagin's Word movement, he changed the name of the church and grew its membership from seventy-five. Today, his church services are televised on multiple television stations, as are many of the services of these Word preachers.

I attended the pretelecast service where the business of the home-based congregation occurs. This early service is different from the timed-out, staged, and concise televised program. But Thompson's church is not yet at slick as Dollar's and is more transparent.

Leroy Thompson's church exterior resembles a warehouse or an old-fashioned sound stage, made of corrugated metal. The surrounding grounds are highly manicured, but the sense of entering a stage set is clear when entering the lobby, which is hung with two massive chandeliers. Masses of flowers give the impression of walking into a place of wealth, but it is only an image. The marble columns? Contact paper. That shiny golden material? Plastic.

The interior of the church resembles a middle school auditorium with a raised staging area at one end and the slogan "Equipping the Body of Christ to Evangelize the World" in gold raised lettering on one wall. But the elaborate camera set-ups among the seating on raised platforms cancel the school image of the auditorium. The intent to tape the event is clear. When I attended, the camera crew began to set up shots during the initial prayer and throughout the preservice, singling out a person who showed emotional piety during prayer, lining up angles for stage shots, getting the choir in focus. In Thompson's church, as in Dollar's, if a white person entered, they were immediately shown to a seat in the front of the auditorium by ushers and targeted by the cameras. The day I attended, there were perhaps five white people present; each of them was seated in front and on screen. Each event from prayer through the preservice became a marking session for taping. Some of these results, especially before the preservice began, could be seen on the huge screens up front as the director called shots and switched cameras. The screens were also used through the service for words to songs and commercials for upcoming church events, such as the pastor's anniversary dinner; judging by the production quality of the commercials, some would be used during the actual broadcast.

As the congregation gathered inside, some individuals prayed in tongues, such prayer being led by a woman on the stage. This charismatic prayer style, glossalalia, is normally a signal of the presence of the Holy Spirit, acting through the person praying. In this case, it became a kind of private prayer, not directed to the community, but a form of meditation. People continued to arrive during this time, and, rather than entering into conversations with other church members, new arrivals quickly began their own prayer in tongues. With seeming cooperation from the Holy Spirit, all glossalalia stopped at five minutes to the prebroadcast session, and congregants moved to their seats.

The service began with several songs, each with simple, repetitive verses that were chantlike. But the use of music is very specific to the theology of Word churches, stressing the principle of positive confession, without "the type of negative thinking and speaking that they find in the traditional songs and hymns of the mainline denominational churches from which so many of them have come."[8] Theological considerations aside, music is centrally important to black church communities, and the excellence with which the music is performed at the Word churches is one of the drawing cards, giving an image of a lively church. Because of its importance, the main musicians are most often paid, not just the directors of the choir and music. The primary band and soloing choir members often are paid and paid very well. There are music ministries open to the congregation, and I suspect that most of those end up in the mass choir toward the back of the stage. The excellence of the music performances is assured. No longer does the congregation suffer through Mrs. Johnson warbling through a hymn, even though her ability to sing praise among a community who knows her also ends. Further, these services are broadcast, and Mrs. Johnson just won't do.

Eventually, Thompson came on the stage. His warm-up message was selectively scripturally based and interpreted in a narrow frame. His folksy, down-home style of presentation was that of an instructing father figure. For instance, he selected Nehemiah 4:6 about the stories of contention as Jerusalem was being rebuilt. He used the story to demonstrate that, as he stated, "A man's soul can be trapped by another man's mouth." From this, Thompson admonished the membership to bring in new people, emphasizing his point with the statement, "Sometimes I got to hurt you to help you."

He used Genesis 4:3 and 4 to compare the difference between God's acceptance of Abel's offering and rejection of Cain's. The difference, Thompson contended, was that Abel brought the *firstling of* his flock, which means that it was the first. So, in like manner, he concluded, the first of any financial advantage should be brought in offering. This offering is different from the tithe. To bring it to the altar for the minister's blessing will ensure that more will follow. Thompson underlined this idea with the statement: "I will not be held accountable for no broke person." Tithing and first fruiting are central in this theology and were emphasized repeatedly. (More on the idea of tithing will be discussed in the section on Dollar's church.) The importance of this principle was such that

Thompson made the claim: "I will go down in history as the Father of Finance."

One woman with whom I spoke at this service has been a member at Thompson's church for seventeen years. When I asked why she was a member for so long, she replied: "I was hurting when I came here. And he [Thompson] talks from everyday life." Thompson as a teacher was important to another woman with whom I spoke. "He *teaches*, he's not like other pastors. I learn something new every week."

Thompson's theology, consistent with the Word of Faith theology, is outlined in his book, *Money Cometh to the Body of Christ*.[9] Like the title, there is little subtlety throughout the text. The principles outlined in *Money Cometh* are straightforward but reflect Thompson's folksy style. These principles begin with the often cited scriptural dictum to believe in Jesus Christ and accept salvation. But what *salvation* means in this view is that God wants believers to be wealthy as a sign of confidence in faith. For instance, Thompson states that Jesus was not poor in his ministry.

> I mean, Jesus lived in complete authority over His financial situation. So when it says in Second Corinthians that Jesus became poor, it isn't talking about Jesus' becoming poor when He was here on earth. The Bible says that Jesus had the Spirit without measure (John 3:34). He knew how to flow with his Father! Jesus had no problems in the area of finances. Whatever He needed, He had. . . . We see Him controlling nature by the laws of prosperity.[10]

In this excerpt from the book, Thompson is close to a heretical view of Jesus, no longer fully human, but controlling his presence in a divine and calculating way. This is not a new heresy and has had several appearances over the history of Christianity. Thompson takes his interpretation further, stating:

> In Jesus' death, burial, and resurrection, He took your place in poverty. He took your place in *poverty* so you could take His place in *prosperity*. Jesus took our place in poverty, but He didn't stay there any longer than three days! Having taken on the sinful state of man, He couldn't stand being broke any longer! He came up on the third day! He said, in effect, "Enough of this!" and He arose, victorious over death, hell, and the grave, and over your poverty.[11]

Thompson's interpretations of Jesus' time in the tomb are unique but grounded in and consistent with all his other ideas, which repeat the same theme: God wants true believers to be rich. His interpretations are also considered eisegetical, reading into biblical history sociocultural ideas from this time frame.

The logic of Thompson's interpretations also directly feed into the longing that many black people have turned into a spiritual quest. The longing for acceptance and success in this land is fulfilled in Thompson's interpretation. Or, as the woman I spoke with said, "I was hurting when I came here." The price for this peace is to have a focus on living into prosperity and ignoring all else, like social inequities, because they are not considered to be of God. Because addressing these inequities is deemed inconsequential to a "real" Christian's task, they are not addressed and they multiply. The focused biblical interpretations are expanded and the injustices begin to be seen in the work of Creflo Dollar.

CREFLO (AND TAFFI) DOLLAR

Creflo Dollar's religious organization is much more widely known and probably the most radical of all the black prosperity preachers. He has promoted himself and his ideas very well, as an article in *Essence* magazine, which was directed to an audience of black women, attests.[12] This article was discussed in more detail in chapter 3, but it is worth noting that the tone of the article, even with the author's mild questions, would be attractive to a black woman who was hungry for this kind of answer to her longing.

Creflo Dollar televises worship services, as do many of the Word of Faith preachers. He will often use a gimmick to engage the members of the viewing audience, such as instructing them to put a dollar in their shoe during the time they are waiting on God's financial blessings. Dollar's church is televised from Atlanta, but I know several people who watch one of his telecasts while they are getting ready for their own church services at other places in the country, and yes, put dollars in their shoes.

I attended Dollar's prebroadcast event before the 11 A.M. service. The entire set-up, from the parking lots to the bookstore to the bathrooms, is much more sophisticated than Thompson's. The crowds are larger and so the show begins in the parking lot. Security is in evidence from the moment one arrives on the grounds, beginning with the numerous uniformed Georgia state troopers guarding the parking lot and directing traffic. Cold-eyed men, clearly security, were outside the doors the day I attended, visually patting down each person who entered. Such security was throughout the building, always observing. Dollar's church is not alone in this business of providing security. I know of one security guard, a retired police officer, who works at another Word of Faith church that is smaller than Dollar's. The guard told me that there are nearly thirty trained guards at the smaller church, and five or six of those guards always travel with the pastor. This use of security has become "normal."

Because I arrived early, I had to wait with others outside the closed auditorium doors or wander as much as security allowed. I tried to see as much as I could before the service began. The entire space was constructed of rich materials; there was no contact paper in evidence. The experience is intended to present pictures of wealth everywhere and to help members see how their money is being used. As in many churches, the different ministries were identified by the minister's color-coded uniform. Since I was waiting, I went to the restroom, thinking I would have an opportunity to speak with some members in an unobserved space. But I was mistaken; there is no uncontrolled space in Dollar's church. Several pink-garbed "bathroom" ministers shepherded each person: through the door, to a stall, to a sink, and out the door. Casual conversation was not possible in that setting. I went to the bookstore.

Most of the materials in the store have been produced by Dollar. The materials are in English or Spanish, in written form or on DVD. There is a regularly produced glossy magazine. There were instructions on marriage, on dating, or on being a good woman. There are many musical recordings, including one set aimed at young people, with Dollar on the label with his hat on backwards, with a kind of aging thug look. The available items that were not produced by Dollar were from Word of Faith ministers, particularly the Copelands and Hagin. The items can be purchased with check, credit or debit card, and cash. In addition to the convenience of this store, there are other opportunities to use credit or debit cards at machines in the lobby before the service begins.

When I was able to enter the auditorium, it was obvious that the security presence was even greater in this setting. I had a camera with me and was told to put it away. When I stated that the service had not started, I was told again to put it away or I would be ejected from the auditorium.

The prebroadcast event was much more staged and polished than was Thompson's. I did not feel as if I was ever in a worship service. For instance, the music productions were slickly produced; a variety of sideshows took place, such as the young white girl using semaphore flags during portions of the music. Again, as people were seated under the watchful gaze of security, the few white participants were quickly placed in the front of the audience. Dollar's church, like several of the Word of Faith or other megachurches, cultivates an image as an "international" church, beginning with its name: World Changers Church International. The camera set-up is more sophisticated as well. In addition to the stationary cameras, there was a roving camera person with a hand-held on stage, getting close-ups of a singer's intense facial expression, a musician, or some other broadcast-worthy view. Because this crew had the more sophisticated production value, I often got the impression that one or another of the participants, on stage or in the audience, played to the camera. What does it mean when piety becomes a publicity stunt? Or when a demonstration of faith is used to garner one's fifteen minutes of fame? I had no answer for such questions, but was saddened by the reflection.

Because I announced that I was a new attendee, I was given a visitor's packet. The enclosed pamphlet lists the beliefs of the church. Among those statements is listed that they believe in "giving alms to the poor, sick, homeless, and others in despair." Yet, during the early service, I heard how some of their altruistic efforts were shaped to retain the focus of their denomination.

For instance, they have a program to help single mothers of sons. This program includes taking the sons for outings with men who can serve as father figures. This program also includes a section that helps the mother learn how to "let go of her son." Masculinity is prized and women have a place. The support of patriarchy in this denomination would resonate within African American communities who have long seen gender roles as a method of fitting into the United States' majority culture.[13] The education of black women out of what is criticized as "matriarchal" or "male-castrating" roles into that of the "virtuous" woman is significant in the Dollar ministry. Who can be prosperous if women and the family structure are not as God ordained them? In this arena of constructing gender, Taffi Dollar is not just a silent partner or publicity prop but an active participant, if not a leader.

In one of the magazines, Taffi Dollar defines the virtuous woman using Proverbs 31 as the backdrop for her interpretation. This virtuous woman "is a woman after God's own heart . . . honorable, truthful, intelligent, confident, capable, and supportive. She is also mentally, spiritually, and physically fit. Her primary focus is the well-being of her household."[14] Taffi Dollar continues that a virtuous woman is a "classy lady" who dresses well. She herself was taught to dress by her husband, which she resisted at first. But she said, "As I began to seek God's Word for wisdom, I realized that Creflo was right."[15]

Taffi Dollar further analyzes relationships between wives and husbands, reflecting that, perhaps, had Eve been more "accountable" to Adam, the whole fall from grace might not have happened.[16] Accountability seems to entail willingness to take instruction from a husband. "Instead of nagging your husband, declare to God, and to yourself, that you will help him become better in his areas of challenge. Ask him how you can be a good help and be willing to do what he says; if he says that he would like you to talk less and listen more, do it."[17] And so, Taffi Dollar wrote, "I humbled myself to receive God's instructions and became more accountable to my husband."[18]

The prebroadcast show began, as did Thompson's, with music, both choir and instrumental numbers. Following several songs, a girl about seven or eight years old gave testimony, talking of her wonderful experience in the World Changers School. In her high-pitched child's voice, to a question about what she learned in school she replied: "I'm learning reading, writing, arithmetic, and how to be an entrepreneur." The woman seated behind me stated: "I want my baby in that school."

Then Taffi Dollar led a prayer, exemplifying the submissive, virtuous woman posture she promotes: she never made eye contact with her audience and made a point to say she was *not* giving a sermon. She began prayer with glossalalia, inviting all members of the audience to participate. Throughout the time of prayer, as people were speaking in tongues, Taffi Dollar interspersed with her own tongue talking with very specific messages. For instance, during one of these messages, she said: "We pray for our friend, the vice president (Cheney) and for all in the election. We need you in our government, Lord . . ." and referenced "these last days" as rationale for needing God in government.

After another live song and taped commercial break, Creflo Dollar gave a talk encouraging the self-esteem of the congregation. "Hold your head high, put your shoulders back. . . ." However, this self-esteem is tied to being right before God, and one can only claim this righteousness if one tithes and, after receiving God's financial blessings, gives the first fruits of the blessings back to the church. Dollar is clear that this giving practice is critical. What the pastor does with the money is never a concern of the giver, inferring that giving money to the pastor is the same as giving it to God. During the service, several people came up and presented the pastor with first fruits.

Tithing is central to prosperity theologies and is structurally tied to the righteousness of the believer before God. According to written statements by Dollar, tithing is the bare minimum. Only after the ten percent of gross income has been made can an offering be given that is acceptable to God. Drawing from Malachi, Dollar expressed God's reaction to an unacceptable offering: "Each week you come and give Him a few dollars, and it's a stench in His nostrils. He doesn't want the offering until you have proven to be faithful over the tithe. His attitude is, since you're not giving the tithe, He's not giving you deliverance, prosperity, or peace."[19]

Dollar also had several members stand and come forward who are running for political office in the Atlanta area. He made it a point to say that they are "getting the message out" through these people, echoing the earlier statement by his wife that God is needed in government. Since Cheney was the "friend" mentioned in the first prayer, there may be a link between this church and partisan politics. The neoconservative streak is already clear from the construction of the virtuous woman.

As smoothly as Dollar's empire is presented, there are places where cracks can be seen. I had an opportunity to speak with some of the Dollars' neighbors. The Dollars' custom home was built in a neighborhood where all residents made a covenant that no fences were to be built around any property. Those who bought or built houses in the subdivision agreed to honor the agreement. The Dollars bought a lot at the end of a cul-de-sac. Their custom built house included a huge wrought iron fence with an electronic gate. When neighbors complained, the Dollars used their political influence with the zoning board to insure that their fence was not removed. Riding roughshod over the neighbors does not seem very Christlike. But it made several people willing to tell me many things. For instance, I asked why there was such a need for security and was told that the Dollars feared for their lives after people gave them their savings or when prosperity promises never happened. I was told that the Dollars are so fearful that they have two houses and as a matter of security never tell anyone in which they will be staying. I found it interesting that one neighbor was very negative about the Dollars' history of Atlanta housing project childhoods. The cracks in the Dollars' surface are all around them.

IMPACT

Dollar and Thompson freely draw from white men's theologies and cultural referents but apply them to black people's experiences with black cultural expressions. By doing so, they creatively address the spiritual longing that black people have had by promising a secure path that will give them all that they have ever wanted materially. These preachers reinterpret Scripture to affirm their central tenet of God's promise of prosperity and that God's love is expected to be made manifest in *this* life. They assist their religious communities' development by using worship to express a sense of unrestrained joy at life's possibilities. Public piety in megachurch settings keeps communities from becoming too intimate and prevents people from asking too many questions; therefore, the communities are more easily controllable. The book and DVD sales help to advance their ideas, controlling the religious education of the members. The closed argument that the ability to understand God's real meaning may be hindered by seminary education helps to limit the conversation partners of the members.

Dollar's church stresses a sense of international connection, never stating that they are a black church and therefore never accountable to black communities. The sense of the international also adds to the glamour, helping black members feel that they are bigger than a simple black church.

Racial analysis, a line of thinking typically addressed in black church life, is deliberately missing from Word of Faith theologies, because it is considered unimportant. In their view, racism is not important because the individual and the desire for money is all that is important. The poor are blamed for their poverty, the poverty itself seen as evidence that they do not fully believe Christ. With money, all seeming injustices can be corrected. Justice is just another commodity in these theologies.

But the one notable break with the lock-step of the Word of Faith organization, because of race, occurred with Fred Price from Los Angeles. Price has long been affiliated with the Hagin/Copeland group and has been a vocal proponent of Word of Faith theology. Price's church is the Crenshaw Christian Center in Los Angeles, which has more than eighteen thousand members.

A few years ago, Price began to critique the racism in the organization after a 1993 comment by Kenneth Hagin Jr., that "when he found one of his children playing with a black friend, he told his child: 'We play. We go together as a group, but we do not date one another.'" Hagin never retracted the idea of separate races, although he did apologize for "hurting" Price.[20] But Price was not satisfied. Price began writing and preaching about the history of racism in Christianity. In an excerpt from the first of three volumes, Price even tells how racism was interwoven in his own faith story. In the 1960s, he attended a tent revival where he had a conversion experience. After the service, a white minister took him and the other converts aside for counseling. Price asked the counselor about Jesus, the answer to all human problems:

"Yet everything about Him is racially segregated. Is heaven going to be like that?" . . . He took the Bible and showed me from the Scriptures—interpreting them in his own way—that it was God's will for the races to be separated. . . . How many generations of blacks have believed that they are cursed and inferior to the rest of mankind? . . . Black people in America have been taught to believe that the white man has all the answers and that black people know nothing.[21]

The core values behind Word of Faith are not obvious, masked by the glitz that seems to offer a share in riches. The relationship with racism is one aspect that became clear to Price. As he became angry about a single incident, he was able to analyze his experiences of religious discrimination and view how racism has been built into Christianity. His response to Hagin's comment exposes one of the fault lines of the Word of Faith. Another value (and fault line) that has yet to be exposed is the solid connection between Word of Faith and politically conservative groups who support ideas and activities that are not actually for the benefit of poor black people.

The theologies that drive these churches of prosperity do indeed give folks fast access to a sense of personal power and self-esteem. The lessons taught imbue the listeners with hope. However, all that is offered is a form of false security against daily threats. There is more on this in my final chapter. For now, we turn to another expression of prosperity churches

6 | METAPHYSICALLY SPEAKING OF PROSPERITY (AND GENDER)

In chapter 4, I distinguished historic black forms of prosperity preaching and in chapter 5 examined the Word of Faith line of prosperity preaching in black communities. The third type of black prosperity churches derives from the Science of Mind and Unity churches. Science of Mind and Unity have "name it and claim it" aspects but are distinctive from the Word of Faith theologies. In some ways, these churches are more difficult to discuss: while Christianity is generally familiar to many, Science of Mind and Unity theologies are sometimes viewed as twisted Christianity, often dismissed as cults, and ultimately given little attention.

The two groups, as was mentioned in chapter 4, derive from the thinking of Phineas Quimby. Charles and Myrtle Fillmore subsequently developed Unity in 1903 and this lineage led to a group of black women developing significant ministries, exemplified by Johnnie Colemon (Chicago) and Barbara King (Atlanta). Ernest Holmes developed Science of Mind in 1927 and from his lineage "Rev. Ike" (New York City and Boston) began ministries.

While they are similar because of Quimby's ideas as their point of origin, I make some distinctions because they differently influence black communities. I begin each section looking at history and theologies, and then move to ministries in black communities.

UNITY: History and Theology

Charles and Myrtle Fillmore, the founders of Unity, were born in the mid-1800s and married in 1881. Myrtle was miraculously healed after praying, "I am a child of God, and therefore I do not inherit sickness."[1] The Fillmores studied other religions such as Buddhism to begin to develop their theology. By 1903, the Unity Society of Practical Christianity had begun in Kansas City, Missouri. Two things from their history are of note for the current day, which also indicate the different ways that Unity operates.

In 1919, the Fillmores began purchasing land for the Unity Village in Missouri where classes and retreats have continued. Today, a variety of programs are offered at Unity Institute, including those that culminate in a Master of Divinity, Master of Arts in Religious Studies, or a Certificate in Unity Ministry. Although the Institute is not accredited at this writing, the courses are offered online, prepare ministers for the denomination, and fill a niche for those who want to study within that theology. Through the Institute and the Unity churches, Unity functions as a religious denomination.

In 1924, the *Unity Daily Word* (renamed the *Daily Word*) was first published. This pamphlet, which provides an easily read, short meditation for each day of the year, is mailed directly to subscribers. A year's subscription is only $12.95. In this and other ways, Unity is nondenominationally directed to all people for their spiritual growth. The *Daily Word* is sometimes found in black homes, located in a place where a moment of reflection can be had. Unity is not evangelistic, so those who regularly use the *Daily Word* can be of any denomination.

The Unity theology has been described as metaphysical, that is, focused upon the connections of spirit and human life, understanding the underlying meanings in life, with a belief that the mind controls the body. Unity lists five basic teachings, which can be found on their website, paraphrased as follows:

1. God is the source and creator of all. There is no other enduring power.
2. We are spiritual beings, created in God's image. The spirit of God lives within each person; therefore, all people are inherently good.
3. We create our life experiences through our way of thinking.
4. There is power in affirmative prayer, which we believe increases our connection to God.
5. Knowledge of these spiritual principles is not enough. We must live them.[2]

Prosperity thinking enters into the basic beliefs of Unity theology: if we create our own realities through thinking, we can create wealth by thinking in terms of abundance. Or we can create conditions of poverty and struggle by always thinking in terms of lack. But prosperity is just one of the aspects of life to create. Using prayer, the good of the moment and life are affirmed; therefore, the major prayer style of Unity is called affirmative prayer. Such affirmations are not prescribed by the church, but are personally designed to fit each person's needs for health, work, money, and so on. Unity defines itself as a biblically based religion, but its interpretations of scripture are distinct, stressing that the basic five principles are themselves scripturally based. Some of this use of scripture will be explored further in the next section.

The importance of a person's mind power to control the perceptions of a situation was told to me in story form by a person from Unity. In the story, three women are sent to hell. The first two women sit around complaining: "We're in hell. . . . Isn't it hot? . . . Don't you hate it here?" Finally they look at the third woman who is just sitting and smiling. "What's wrong with you?" the first two women ask. "Don't you know you're in hell?" To which the third woman replies: "I'm not." The third woman in the story is an example of a Unity student. Members will often refer to themselves as "students" who are always working to develop a life that is not defined by a given situation. The point of the story emphasizes this aspect, not the hell portion; the idea of a literal heaven or hell is not so much a future occurrence, but something we each create on earth. Complaining about a situation is not the Unity way of dealing with it. Life situations must be dealt with, and the mind is the place to begin.

JOHNNIE COLEMON AND BARBARA KING

Johnnie Colemon's church in Chicago is the Christ Universal Temple for Better Living, or CUT, with a membership of approximately four thousand. Her beginnings are described in this way:

> After learning she had an incurable disease (1953), Johnnie enrolled in the Unity School of Christianity in Lee's Summit, Missouri, where she received her teaching certificate and became an ordained minister. Always a trailblazer, Dr. Colemon pio-

neered many "firsts" while at Unity—the first black to live at Unity Village and the first to have been elected as president of the Association of Unity Churches.[3]

But in 1974, Colemon broke her congregation's direct affiliation with Unity because of her own continual experiences of racism.[4] One long-time black member of another Unity church told of this break with a sense of pride. Colemon, according to the story, fought the racism within Unity from the time of her studies in the Unity Institute. She built alliances with a few other white Unity ministers, ultimately changing the organization. With a new direction in 1974, CUT was named an Independent New Thought Church. The idea of "new thought" church communities was an outgrowth that would come to encompass Unity, Religious Science, and any related churches. But Colemon's relationship with the Association of Unity Churches was by no means the end of her work with Unity theology.

Colemon also began the Universal Foundation for Better Living with an international focus on education and spirituality that has resulted in the establishment of over thirty affiliated churches. "The UFBL Inc. is an international organization of independent New Thought (metaphysical) Christian churches, founded by Dr. Colemon in June 1974 and committed to spreading the abundant-living message of Jesus Christ throughout the world."[5]

Despite what appears to be an evangelical phrase, "spreading the message," other material from Colemon clarifies her sense of "spreading":

> We hold a positive thought about the world; we pray for people and conditions and give thanks for light. We make no effort to try to convert friends or loved ones; we simply make the Truth ideas available and leave people to find the Truth for themselves. At Christ Universal Temple, we aspire to be a spiritual center in which the message of Jesus the Christ is interpreted and modeled in a relevant and practical way to attract diverse ethnic and cultural communities. We do not attempt to teach you what to think, but rather how to think.[6]

Supporting this international structure is the Johnnie Colemon Theological Seminary in Florida, which offers UFBL teacher and minister preparation courses, including courses for previously ordained ministers, and a Master of Divinity degree.[7] In addition to courses in scriptural and theological studies and Koine Greek, there is a course in Fillmorian theology, indicating the connection with the Unity line of thought. Most of the courses are available online.

When I visited the Christ Universal Temple, Colemon was not there. That did not deter people from coming for worship. There were quite a few older black folks there, perhaps an indication of the number of years that Colemon has been ministering in Chicago. I was unable to find a current picture of Colemon; most were clearly taken when she was younger. Perhaps the young and vital photograph serves as a kind of icon for the membership. They are to understand her as the founder.

The atmosphere at the church was relaxed and it was clear that people had a different sense of community than did the Word of Faith churches I visited. One indication of this was in the church bulletin, where the notice of the annual membership meeting was given. Two items on the agenda were the election of the board of directors and a financial report to be given by an independent accounting firm. The notice included a word to those who are friends of CUT but not members: welcome to attend the annual meeting, but not able to vote. The openness of this invitation and the clarity about funds would give members a great sense of "this church is mine."

And people displayed their ownership of the space. The community was generally welcoming. If I looked lost, most were quick to offer assistance. When I visited the bookstore, several people helped me find compact discs of Johnnie Colemon's sermons. It seems that sermons of the week are recorded and available for sale after the services. But it had been some time since Colemon had been there preaching, and few copies were left. The compact discs were not specifically about prosperity, but included her preaching on other topics. The compact discs had a major advantage over printed material: I was able to hear her preaching and the delivery of her message. Colemon was clearly delivering her sermons in the style of a black preacher. Some of her preaching was accompanied by an organ playing softly in the background. All of the recorded preaching was with call-and-response exchanges with her listeners. Occasionally, she would make a statement several times and have her listeners repeat all or some of the words back to her. Such repetition is not new to black church communities but Colemon's usage was more instructive. She made the point in her writing:

> There is something peculiar about this ministry that makes it extremely wonderful to me. It is a teaching ministry; I like it because it teaches you what to do. We teach you how to live a better life. I share with you what I believe, and what I have discovered that will work in your life. . . . Some of this might be a new thought to you, and that's what we're called—a New Thought ministry. . . . If what you have been using all these years has not worked for you, then it is time for a new thought. That's why I changed. I went into the New Thought movement because I'd been in "church" all my life . . . and I always walked out the same way I was when I went in there. They used great, big, beautiful words, and they sounded wonderful, but I never really knew what they were talking about.[8]

Colemon's approach to prosperity preaching is covered in a set of workbooks, *It Works If You Work It*. The first chapter is "There is only One Presence. Claim your Divine inheritance! It's a sin to be poor."[9] The sin and poverty references may seem to be the equivalent of Word of Faith, but it is not, because God is viewed differently. In the UFBL/Unity theology, God is all good and nothing but good comes from God. The things we dislike in life, like poverty, do not come from God but from our own mind, our sin of buying into a poor consciousness. When we claim our divine inheritance, we begin to draw riches to us. "The work begins in your mind. . . . You have to be willing to try to think only positive, rich, abundant thoughts. . . . You are going to bless that pocketbook and think—PLENTY! . . . If you are experiencing fear, remember that fear does not come from God."[10]

Colemon's definitions of prosperity also need clarification. Whereas the Word group measured success in terms of money and things, Colemon states, "Anytime I say the word 'prosperity,' the majority of people think I am talking about money. But what does prosperity really include? Health, love, peace of mind, all that God is, all the good things of life."[11] Colemon also emphasizes that God is the substance under all things, and this includes money. "This God-substance is all around each one of us, waiting for us to form, mold, and shape it into whatever we want."[12]

It is not until the second volume of the series that Colemon mentions tithing as part of the scriptural, universal laws but, she claims, many ministers do not teach it because they are afraid.

> The first thing the congregation will say is that you are up there talking just for the money. But I'm not. I'm a tither and whether you know it or not, this church tithes. . . . Tithing is the secret of prosperity, the secret of your success. I have given it to you and I hope that you will use it because I want you to be what God has created you to be—rich, happy, and good-looking.[13]

Colemon's discussion of tithing is brief and limited rather than the center of the theology she preaches.

Colemon's Unity-based thinking has often been collapsed into the Word of Faith preaching. For example, one writer states: "New Thought metaphysical teachings, synthesized with charismatic Christianity, are *the ideological basis for today's Word of Faith movement*. Thus, Colemon should be thought of as a forerunner of the contemporary African American Faith teachers."[14] While Colemon may have inspired others, I would argue that her success in teaching a nontraditional black Christian point of view was a more important inspiration to the development of preachers like Dollar and Thompson. It was much less her theology than her use of black traditional worship forms in communicating different religious views that was critical. If her theology were taken into account, the openness to women pastors would also be important.

Johnnie Colemon has been notable in developing the ministry of black women through the UFBL. This is no small feat in light of the number of black women still playing a submissive role in churches, as Taffi Dollar demonstrated from her not-a-sermon time in the pulpit. Darnise Martin reflected on the strong presence of women in UFBL: "A look at the affiliated church list shows that only one [of the churches] is not led by a woman. Interestingly, the list also includes a church in Los Angeles headed by the well-known actress Della Reese."[15]

Colemon may be more widely well-known in some ways, such as growing the UFBL and its affiliates. But Barbara King is also an established presence in the Atlanta area. King established the Hillside Chapel and Truth Center in 1971 with twelve members in her living room, as it states on her website biography.[16] Today, that church has ten thousand members and "was the first African-American New Thought affiliate to establish a sister-church in South Africa. The South African branch was ordained in 1994."[17]

King's connection with Unity theology is not drawn in as clear a set of lines as was Colemon's. But there are similarities to Colemon's story.

> Overcoming a life-threatening physical condition as a teenager, Barbara was inspired to live by increasing her faith in God in her to heal any condition. . . . She holds a bachelor's degree in sociology, a master's degree and certification in social work, several honorary doctorates in divinity, and a number of years of training in religion and the ministry. . . . This independent church is an ecumenical ministry, a new thinking church, founded on the teachings of Jesus Christ and the practical application of His Principles to everyday living.[18]

This statement, emphasizing the church's independence and never naming the locations of religious training, set up a great distance from Unity. This same nebulous identification is part of the program at Barbara King School of Ministry, where enrichment classes in reiki and auto repair are mixed in with Aramaic Bible study and a prosperity class.

Yet the relationships to Unity and Fillmore's thought are clear in King's theology as seen in her discussions of prosperity, outlined in her book, *Transform Your Life*. King uses the biblical story of Jesus turning water into wine to outline how each person can change a life situation they do not like. For King, this story illustrates how Jesus demonstrates the Truth of human capabilities and power. To make a change, there must first be a vision of what shape one desires her life to take. While God has authority over all, each person must be enabled to use good judgment and to begin to create what she or he wants. The image of water-into-wine is used metaphysically, King states, with the parenthetical comment: "If at some point you turn physical water into physical wine, please write me at once!"[19] It is also important, she counsels to remain calm in the face of life situations. Panic only creates negative mind-sets. "We sometimes become so negative that we are submerged in the waters of negation."[20]

King also clarifies her definition of the word prosperity.

> When we use the word prosperity, we're talking about health. We are talking about peace of mind—a sense of well-being. We are also talking about what most often comes to mind at the mention of prosperity—financial, material, and social stability. In other words, we are talking about all the wealth, all the goodness that God is. When we recognize that prosperity covers all of these areas of our lives, we will begin to realize that it must have a spiritual basis. Prosperity brings vitality.[21]

The second step in the process is to be grateful for what is already in one's life, no matter how small. What we have is already from God, so we should not be ungrateful. We must think of problems as challenges and then opportunities. Next, there must be no doubt that the desired outcome will be achieved. There may be a waiting period, but this should not deter the believer.

> No matter how long you may have to wait for your good, when it comes, it will always come in abundance . . . perhaps it just isn't time for it to be revealed to you. Your job is to keep trusting. During the time you are waiting, you can prove the Lord. Always keep in mind the vision of your desired outcome."[22]

In addition to these basic steps, King lays out five other instructions to achieve prosperity.

> You have to know that you don't depend on other persons or conditions for your prosperity. . . . You have to let go of worn-out ideas, worn-out conditions, worn-out relationships. . . . The act of release [of negative thinking] is magnetic. . . . You must forgive all that has offended you, within and without. . . . . Do the work you love, and love the work you do.[23]

This section is a reminder that the theology presented by King, like Colemon's and other thinkers' in the Fillmore line, is indeed practical. The five instructions are in the vein of common sense, but this approach is integral to the theology. King's book covers multiple areas of life concern, such as dealing with fear, death, or love relationships, with the same mixture of scripture, reflection, humor, and common sense. At the end of each section, King also offers sample affirmations that can be used as the person works on her or his state of mind. Some of the affirmations for prosperity are: "God is the source of my supply," "I am never without money (health, friends)," or "My Heavenly Father's good is always available to me."[24]

Barbara King's ideas are very closely aligned with those of Unity, as this usage of affirmations to remove negative and allow only positive thoughts demonstrates. This stress on the mind is also part of the Science of Mind group, but takes a bit of a different turn.

SCIENCE OF MIND THEOLOGY

Ernest Holmes did not intend to begin a church. He was a self-taught man, having quit school when he was fifteen, returning only to study public speaking. He searched for meaning in his personal studies, looking for truth, exploring literature, art, science, philosophy, and religion. At one point, he encountered some Christian Scientists and studied their thinking as well,

> especially about the healings they believed possible by those who prayed a certain way. If such things were possible to them, he reasoned, such things must also be possible to others. Long afterward, [Holmes] elaborated on this reaction: "Anything anyone has ever done, anybody can do; there can be no secrets in nature. This I have always believed. There is no special providence, no God who says, 'I am going to tell you what I didn't tell any others.'"[25]

These atheistic leanings are an important part of Holmes' theology. In the Unity tradition, the Jesus/Christ/God figures are real, even though the Christ-God in each person is the source of power. But in Religious Science, this God/human division is erased.

Darnise Martin's extensive ethnographic study of a black Religious Science church in California elaborates on this teaching about God.

> The church teaches that the entire universe has been created good, and each human being is God in the flesh. Refuting the idea

of a distant God, they claim instead that God is within. . . .
Members believe that Jesus' birth story should be understood
metaphysically as the story of every person. . . . Indwelling divinity is based upon the Science of Mind teaching that each person
is an individualized expression of God, who therefore embodies
the divine in human form. In turn, this value supports the idea
that a life of well-being and abundance is normative.[26]

In 1927, Holmes developed the Science of Mind and, at the urg-
ings of friends, established the Institute of Religious Science and
School of Philosophy in Los Angeles. Today, Religious Science is
taught from the Holmes Institute in Burbank, California. The graduate program is rigorous and designed for spiritual leaders. The
United Church of Religious Science is only open to those who have
reached, or nearly so, the educational level of "Licensed Practitioner."
To enter the program, students are also expected to have a bachelor
degree, unless given a special waiver. Psychology, administration, religion, education, and quantum physics are included in the program.
Most faculty have advanced degrees, if not doctorates, from U.S.
schools such as the Pacific School of Religion, schools within the
University of California system, the University of Michigan, and international schools, including Calcutta University and the University
of Innsbruck. The Distance Education and Training Council accredited the school in 2003.

The basic practice of the religion follows the affirmative prayer
pattern described by Colemon and King. But the process itself is not
dogmatically prescribed. Martin reported that in the congregation
she attended, Holmes' words on Religious Science are on the front
cover of the church's weekly program. "Religious Science is a corre-
lation of the Laws of Science, Opinions of Philosophy, and revela-
tions of Religion applied to human needs and the aspirations of
man."[27] These same ideas are reflected in Rev. Ike's Harlem church.

REV. IKE

I attended a Sunday afternoon healing and blessing meeting at Rev.
Ike's Harlem church. The church is the Palace Cathedral, a former
movie theater that covers an entire block. The church building has
an air of fading glory; unlike the other churches I visited, this was

not a shiny new building. Since it had been a movie theater, there were plenty of places to paint with gold and red, giving an overall flamboyant appearance. The afternoon session was not held in the theater section, but in a smaller room to accommodate the small group of worshippers. Of the fifty or so people attending the service, the majority were older, mostly women and some men. The ministers were men and women; leadership was shared. The service, which did not last long, was a time of song, community announcements, a sermon, a collection, and time for reflection. Book sales took place in the back of the chapel at a table set up by the bookstore manager.

Frederick Eikerenkoetter—Rev. Ike—embraces the Science theology. For instance, the discussion of who God is in this theology is reflected in some of his writing as he defines Jesus as limited by other definitions:

> The meek and mild concept is what I call the "Sunday School Jesus." . . . To some people, Jesus was a man on earth two thousand years ago, who is coming again "some day." But I say that Jesus represents the ever-living Presence of God within. I'd like to share with you the Science of Living definition of Jesus Christ. Christ is the Presence of God-in-man—every man. Jesus is the only one who perfectly demonstrated the Christ. But it is not enough for Jesus to be the ONLY one to realize and demonstrate the Christ. Each man must come to know the truth of his own Christhood.[28]

But this stated theology did not align with one of the songs sung by the congregation at the service. The words of the hymn, "Trust and Obey," could be sung in any Christian church: "When we walk with the Lord in the light of his word, / What a glory he sheds on our way! / While we do his good will, he abides with us still, / And all with all who trust and obey."[29] At the same time that Eikerenkoetter defines his theology, he offers blessed prayer cloths in his magazine and sales catalog. These prayer cloths, which are sometimes found at revivals or in charismatic churches, are used for specific requests such as getting health or money. In addition, Eikerenkoetter's advertisement for the cloths claims "Evil influences and 'crossed conditions' are being removed." The instructions to use the cloth are to "think in your mind that it represents me, a Man of God, laying my hands upon you and praying the prayer of faith for you."[30] Does Eikerenkoetter counter his stated theological beliefs when he sells prayer cloths? Does this mixture of gimmicks and more traditional Christian worship, such as the hymn, help attract and retain black people to his church's membership? This process of blending a given theology with other religions' ideas and with specific cultural practices is not new in black communities; however, the process seems to have been raised up a notch in Eikerenkoetter's development of his churches. However, in his earlier writings, the connection with Religious Science was clear.

In a 1972 Science of Living Study Guide, produced by Eikerenkoetter, each lesson had an exposition, commentary, and a section called "Come Now, Let Us Reason Together." These reasoning exercises are sets of questions, such as "What is the purpose of prayer and meditation? What constitutes successful prayer?" This question section is followed by affirmative treatments. Following the questions about prayer, the affirmations are: "As I look into the mirror of my Inner Self I behold the Father-in-me. I acknowledge His Almighty, All-Powerful Presence as the Truth of me."[31] Unlike Colemon, who remained centered in Unity thought, the development of Eikerenkoetter's theology took another, less educated turn.

When I attended the service, Eikerenkoetter was not physically present; I did not expect it because his base church is in Boston. However, the church community clearly identified with him as founder and leader. His photo was everywhere and, in some places, photos of "Rev. Mrs. Ike" and their son Bishop Xavier Frederick Eikerenkoetter could also be seen.

Eikerenkoetter's age is another issue. Frederick Eikerenkoetter was born in 1935, beginning his ministry career in his home state of South Carolina. As at Colemon's church, there were no current photos of Eikerenkoetter evident at his church, but there are many photos of a younger Eikerenkoetter with a black men's hair style that is seldom seen today, processed and pomaded looking. According to *Miracles Right Now!* magazine and sales catalog, Eikerenkoetter has celebrated his fiftieth anniversary in ministry. The church in South Carolina where he began as an assistant pastor is not Religious

Science, but is a charismatic, evangelistic congregation. It is not clear when he moved to Religious Science. His doctorate may have come from a Science of Living course (D.Sc.L.?) He has established the United Christian Evangelistic Association in Boston and the Christ Community United Church in New York, its services held in the Palace Cathedral. But Eikerenkoetter embraced the Religious Science theology. Yet he did not stop there, even as he mixed it with scriptural quotes and some popular religious gimmicks as described previously. The same mixture can be seen in his prosperity preaching.

In his Science of Living study guide (enhanced with a sticker proclaiming "Fried Chicken for the Soul"), Eikerenkoetter states that many religious people do not realize that we should make "peace with money. For money comes to you through your mind. Everything comes to you through your own mind."[32] To claim to be poor for Christ's sake is wrong, because no child of God should experience lack. But, he cautions,

> Be sure to keep your relationship with money balanced. You must let money know point blank that you love it and understand what the relationship is. And you must get to the point where money loves you. That's when your mind is really money-conditioned. . . . Every time you look around, here comes more money. . . . I like the way the Bible expresses overflowing abundance in the 23rd Psalm, the 5th verse. . . . "My cup runs over." That tells me that people who serve God ought to have overflowing abundance.[33]

While this statement focuses on the control of the mind to create one's situation, there is another publication by Eikerenkoetter that has little sophistication about seeking prosperity. He does not use his full name on this one, just the title "Rev. Ike." Perhaps that is a way for the publication geared to more serious study is distinguished from more popular religion productions.

On a nine-by-four-inch coupon-format booklet, a glossy cover is styled like a thousand dollar bill, with one of the older photos of Rev. Ike in the center. With a heading "Money answers all things" and a quote from the Rev.—"The LACK of money is the root of all evil!"—the booklet promises to show how money, prosperity, and success seeds can be planted. The first pages of the booklet are anecdotes of people who have achieved their dreams by following Rev. Ike's instructions:

> As I walked down the aisles in Philadelphia at my Meeting, a lady spoke these words into my ear: "Rev. Ike, I'm now a Black Millionaire!" I replied to her: "Honey, you are now a GREEN millionaire. Color of skin has nothing to do with the color of money! In the American economy, the color of Power is Green." She and I rejoiced together about that. She sends me regular Money Seed donations on the Blessing Plan.[34]

The Blessing Plan of the booklet is contained in the second part, which has twelve coupons to be mailed to the Boston church with "seeds" of twenty to one hundred dollars. The seeds are to grow into miracle money. The instructions are clear. Before the twelve coupons are finished, make sure to send for another booklet.

> A lady said, "Rev. Ike, when should I stop working with the Blessing Plan?" I said, "Lady, whenever you want your blessings to STOP, then and only then STOP with the Blessing Plan." She said, "Then I won't EVER STOP!" Don't let anyone know that you are working with the Miracle Money book unless you are more than sure that they will not give you static about it.[35]

Rev. Ike or Frederick Eikerenkoetter does not really align with the theology of Religious Science any longer. He may have begun there, but he seems to have strayed. Rev. Ike may also be the inspiration for another generation of unclear religious thought.

"Master Prophet" Bernard Jordan is also around the New York City area and is buying television time on the BET cable network. He began his ministry in the late 1980s and today runs a traveling "Prophecology" conference, attracting new prophets for his Prophetic Order of Mar Elijah (P.O.M.E.). The definition of the prophet used by Jordan draws from the common or popular reference to the fortuneteller or soothsayer; the biblical use of prophet is one who calls the people back to God. But Jordan's advertisement for his conference sets out prophets as precognitives: "Discover the fundamentals of vital metaphysical truths in the operation of the prophetic. Engage in powerful, life-changing workshops. Experience the power of God in nightly Mircle [sic] Services, where the prophets will prophesy to your situation." On his website (www.BishopJordan.com), he states that he has already attracted three hundred prophets. The metaphysical, without the troubling aspects of denominational affiliations or guidelines, can be very profitable, it seems.

NEW THOUGHT RELIGIONS

These types of religion are often classed under the title of the metaphysical. This is an older term that is being replaced by the term New Thought religions. All these forms are sometimes grouped together and considered a "movement," the New Thought movement, but that term is not precise. When these titles are used, we often lose clarity that the theologies of Unity and Religious Science are not the same despite their similarities. By grouping them together, distinctions between the religions are lost and so hybridized versions are further muddied in our understandings. Since the Internet and television are being utilized to rapidly spread information about these new forms of religion and to entice potential new members, it is in our collective best interests to be able to grasp the concepts used by the religions, which are different from, but communicating with, Christian concepts.

Yet there are New Thought organizations beginning to bring members of Unity and Religious Science together for conversations and sometimes conferences. One that is of note is the International New Thought Alliance, one of the older associations serving as a kind of clearinghouse and bringing these various metaphysical religions together for annual conferences.

Another similar organization, and one of greater note with regard to African Americans, is the Association for Global New Thought. This organization seeks "planetary healing," which the members see as a natural outcome of metaphysical, positive thinking. Two of the organization's board members are African American leaders in this thinking. Argentina Glasgow is the leader of the Detroit Unity Temple, with a primarily African American congregation. She is also on the Executive Board for the Association of Unity Churches, so her leadership has national implications. The Detroit Unity Temple has been a significant source for the development of other black leaders in Unity. Another board member with the Association for Global New Thought is Michael Beckwith, founder of the Agape International Spiritual Center near Los Angeles, a Religious Science church. Beckwith is involved on a national level with the United Church of Religious Science.

A source document for the Association for Global New Thought is included on its website. This "Declaration of Our Awakened World" applies positive thinking to the world's situation, including its prosperity:

> Religious traditions are understood as cultural perceptions of the Divine that have led the world into a trans-denominational convergence. . . . We now see that true profit is the benign impact that our choices have on future generations. Our first priority is the benefit afforded to the Whole System. Our wise choices have resulted in the renewal and restoration of the Earth's natural ecology and her resources. We honor our planet as the Mother body which gives us our daily bread. Global resources are shared by all, eliminating the concepts of "first and third" worlds. Ethnocentric nationalism fades away as Spiritual communities take root. . . . The concept of violence is nonexistent in our consciousness and therefore our world. We have shifted from weaponry to creativity. . . . Our spiritual understanding has brought forth a natural prosperity proving the Truth that abundance is our birthright.[36]

This philosophy is very different from the grasping view of Rev. Ike or the closed theology of Word of Faith. It represents an opportunity wherein African Americans could continue to address a spirituality of longing, work with others in black churches, and yet focus on social justice in a global framework. This focus combines individual thinking with a global consciousness, a direction that may be seen in other metaphysical churches. This organization may represent a sign of things to come in the development of some metaphysical theologies and provides a point of contrast.

Darnise Martin characterized the significance of New Thought for African Americans in this way:

> New Thought provides tools for individual empowerment. This differs significantly from the communal emphasis of the tradi-

tional black religions. The teachings are centered on personal up-
lift, personal empowerment, and personal achievement through
the raising of individual consciousness. The philosophy does not
overly seek to answer questions of worldwide suffering or
poverty. Individual concerns appear to be elevated over the concerns of the community. For African Americans, this would seem
to be a divergence from historical cultural norms that still reflect
an African worldview which seeks the welfare of the community
over the individual.[37]

Beyond the ideas that Martin identifies, the worldwide consciousness of the Association of Global New Thought may represent a development that signals a new direction that will ultimately attract
many other black people to participate in these metaphysical religions. While some black Americans may like the promise of quick
cash through religion, and others may prefer the focus on self, the
addition of a global vision may be a greater lure. There is still one
question that has yet to be addressed directly in this chapter: What
factors might attract black Americans to participate in metaphysical
religions?

ATTRACTING BLACK MEMBERS

In the second chapter, I discuss a black spirituality of longing and
contend that the metaphysical strands of religion—Unity, Religious
Science, UFBL, Christ Community United Church, and even
Prophecology—may be attractive to African Americans for another
reason: The ideas are not new in black communities.

I came to understand this frustration about everything-old-is-
new-again after hearing several white scholars dismiss black folks'
work in hoodoo as just another form of metaphysical thinking. At
other times, I have heard stories about racism in training ministers
for Unity churches: these stories seem to revolve around how
African Americans' culturally derived concepts might be related to
concepts that are taught as invented by Fillmore.

In 2004, I interviewed a black folk healer, Sakoura. Having studied widely, she still expressed anger over the way many white religious thinkers and healers never gave credit to their sources of information. She had some sharp words to use about "metaphysicians."

What a lot of white scholars and students of so-called meta-physics are calling "metaphysics" is the retentions of indigenous peoples' work. It's African, Native American, and Asian peoples' work, re-worked and put into another language. It's culture theft, that's what it is. What people are calling metaphysics was First People's worldview to begin with. What they're calling meta-physics is really a way of saying "You people don't have anything, you just trying to do a knockoff." It was our work to begin with. All you have to do is look at where people are going to study, when they decide they are going to claim their authenticity. They go to Kenya. They go study with Native American peoples.

The metaphysical ideas that are presented may resonate with black Americans for many reasons. The religious thinking in Unity or Religious Science offers belief in possibilities, beyond the seem-ing limits of a given moment. If there is a spirituality of longing in the heart of a black person, this thought can give a rational way to define how mind power will work to present solutions.

The idea of possibilities and the power of the mind are ideas at the core of spirituality and other aspects of black mystical traditions. Where black Catholics could use their professed Christian religious base to dream of new applications of cultural religious ideas—such as Voudou (New Orleans and Haiti), Candomble (Brazil), or Obeah (Jamaica)—Protestant Christianity offered few spiritual enrich-ments that were easily transferable to new contexts, such as Catholic saints and incense use. Protestant worship under enslavement even forbade the Africans their use of drums. But culture finds ways to live. Hoodoo, with direct links to black cultural concepts of the spir-itual, was practiced throughout the South, and these practices con-tinued as black Americans migrated North. The African-derived cultural concept of a holistic view of the cosmos, where elements were connected and interwoven and able to influence each other, continued among African Americans.

The metaphysical churches under discussion would also be at-tractive to African Americans because they offer a reasoned way to think about a holistic view of the universe. These religions, further, stress the importance of power over the self through the control of the mind: a spirituality of longing would seek the experience of controlling aspects of life in a world that has not often offered black folks command of their own lives.

The prosperity preaching in black communities from the metaphysical/Unity/Religious Science lineage is distinct. To put this in context with other forms of prosperity preaching, the general social influences in black communities need to be considered.

*What if the Negro people be wooed from a strife for righteousness, from
a love of knowing, to regard dollars as the be-all and end-all of life?*
What if to the Mammonism of America be added the rising
Mammonism of the re-born South, and the Mammonism of this
South be reinforced by the budding Mammonism of its half-
wakened black millions? Whither, then, is the new-world quest of
Goodness and Beauty and Truth gone glimmering?[1]

I have tried to bring together many voices of people who consider
aspects of or are involved in prosperity preaching in black communities. Not all the voices speak of religion or race or economics, but
taken together, we have seen that many black intellectual streams
converge regarding prosperity preaching. The opening words from
W. E. B. Du Bois were written long before the prosperity churches
we know today existed. But African American needs for social acceptance and clarity of identity in a hostile land are not new; we
long to be settled, but what is the best direction? Prosperity
churches bring some answers that return to Du Bois's questions.

The previous three chapters deal with the distinctions between
the churches, rather than reducing them into a single category. They
are not the same, but fall along a continuum, presenting different visions of prosperity to black people. In chapter 3, Daddy Grace and
Father Divine are grouped together with Marcus Garvey and James
Forman to demonstrate that there have been historical attempts to
address economic issues through black religious thought. But new
developments occurred, for which the Word of Faith group, discussed in chapter 4, provides an example from within an evangelical
framework. Chapter 5's discussion of metaphysical groups covers a

variety of expressions that address prosperity issues in similar ways, beginning with the human mind. On several levels, the Word of Faith group as well as the metaphysical group reflect the social changes that black U.S. citizens have undergone since the mid-1960s. Throughout these social changes, a black American spirituality of longing with a search for religious fulfillment has been constant. We turn now to the larger social issues that have ensued along with the development of prosperity preaching as it has seeped into the spiritual life of black Americans.

CHASING THE GOOD LIFE

There are many ways to think about the shift in social relations among African Americans themselves and between black and white Americans. We encounter evidence of these new social relations at every turn. Interracial dating and marriage are relatively common, considering attitudes, practices, and laws of even two decades ago. African American men and women are sometimes seen in visible leadership positions that were only dreams twenty years ago. So while once it was radical idea for black men to play the quarterback position in football games, today we can find black men in head coach positions for National Football League teams. Black actresses and actors win awards for a wide array of performances, a far cry from the day of Hattie McDaniel's Oscar for a maid's role. These sights are common for this time, as are the seemingly increased levels of black political participation in the United States. Illinois Senator and presidential hopeful Barack Obama has been referred to as a political "rock star" who appeals to all Americans.

Thus, it is not surprising that race is easily kicked aside as unimportant to understanding social problems; the evidence of a few successes seems to underscore its ending as an American problem. Michael Eric Dyson describes this situation related to black leadership:

> Public figures who call attention to the structural, moral, psychological, social, and cultural factors that preserve white supremacy are not tolerated for long. . . . They are viewed as ethnosaurs, figures who can't let go of race as an explanation of the forces that hurt our nation.[2]

The rejection of race is accompanied by a fully American cultural emphasis on the individual, to the exclusion of the community. The individual can achieve in spite of social constrictions against all odds: this is set out as the rugged American way. Acceptance of the status quo, rather than seeking solutions, becomes the mantra for those who would succeed. These factors become central to the construction of prosperity preaching. Race and oppressive limits are all in your mind and that is not who God created you to be, most will argue. The religious analysis is not to focus on social problems; the analysis must begin with how you commit sin by not being all God created you to be. Race, especially, is unimportant in the grand scheme of focusing on your giftedness and seeking God's material blessings—when, like the Unity story of the three women in hell, you can just ignore the bad things and think positively.

This results in a conflation of positive thinking about individualized importance, with self-esteem added to God's image with a goal of personal gratification. Black theologian Lee Butler refers to this mixture as the reduction of religious life to trends of popular culture.

> Our belief in our humanity and our God continues to be defined by an American Dream of economic prosperity. Human agency, as communicated through popular mass media, is evidenced by every individual's ability to follow a marketing strategy for economic security. . . . By blending an entitling God with the wealth of the earth . . . combining high culture values, "high church" aesthetics, and popular culture "pursuit of happiness," the gospel of prosperity, as the reinterpreted Dream, has created a groundswell. . . . The social gospel of prosperity measures human worth with the Dream as the standard.[3]

However, perhaps Butler's assessment is too harsh. Perhaps it is time for African Americans to step away from race concepts and grow into full Americans. But does that mean, somehow, that black American experiences have not really been *American*? The fallacy is to think that black experiences are less than white experiences and that we have been deprived of some mythical American experience. That fallacy might make sense if there were no poor white people in the United States, some of whom have experienced their own forms of oppression, but supposedly given the comfort of a blanket of white privilege: ultimately, racism has been friend to very few people. The story of racism, with all the subplots of who has been victimized, hated, murdered, abused, denigrated, or ridiculed is a fully American story, riddling the history and muddling the present. If black Americans, who have been one of the main targets of racism, act as if we can transcend or ignore this history, we only play into the hands of those who benefit from continuing racism's legacy. Here, too, is another aspect of a spirituality of longing: many African Americans want to be fully accepted as citizens. "Passing" happens when black people who look white deny being black so that they can be accepted. Passing still happens today, and having white skin is no longer required. I have heard of one brown-skinned man born in the United States who harkens back to an ancestor to proudly state he is Jamaican and is not black. Ward Connerly, a black man in California leading the battles against the "privilege" of affirmative action, chooses to call himself "Irish." These denials of race and racism are revisionist history with denial of those ancestors who did not have the option to "make-believe" their lives. But perhaps, like other social movements in black communities, there is need to think through the implications and consequences of any intellectual stance. Ethicist Garth Baker-Fletcher describes such growth for himself.

> My Africentric awakening was . . . dramatic because I stopped trying to "make it" on the terms, values, and norms assigned by Euro-domination. . . . The fundamental transformation of Africentric awakening is giving oneself permission to enjoy one's Afrikanity, to revel in the beauty and uniqueness of one's Afrikan self, and to develop that self with a fierceness and pride. Such a step of consciousness is transformative because it frees one from trying to dress "right," act "right," look "right," and talk "right." "Rightness" has always been whiteness in the United States. . . . I have come to realize that Afrikans cannot wait for Europeans or any other people to accept us, because it is likely that they never will.[4]

In this view, different from that of prosperity churches, a black racial identity is not denied but embraced. Consciousness in this view involves not just a positive mental state, but also a full acceptance of the self. Both this view and the positive-mindset-prosperity think-ing come from psychological approaches to becoming whole, and both offer coping strategies.

Prosperity preaching generally stresses the individual person's will over history as the God-approved route to overcoming racial op-pression. This preaching will also stress the importance of the indi-vidual over the community. There is irony in such a stance because it is only possible now, after the sacrifices have been made through seg-regation and dehumanization and disenfranchisement. Such a stance does not offer any solutions to continuing racial injustice. One of the ways that prosperity preaching helps to construct new, not-really-black identities is through identification of the church community in global terms. Each of the churches I visited or studied claimed some other church community in a foreign country. In such a way, the con-gregation does not have to deal with questions of being a "black" church; instead it claims an international identity. In prosperity preaching, if denying racism and thinking positive thoughts are im-portant building blocks for new black identities, so are the ways to support the status quo regarding issues of social class and gender.

SOCIAL CLASS, MONEY, LONGING, AND RELIGION

Part of the American wealth fantasy is that money instantly brings about a change in social class, as Rev. Ike's comment that the woman was not a black millionaire but a green one. The fantasy of money is that it provides access to a life of the rich and famous. But this is a misunderstanding of the structure of social class. The United States is not a classless society that determines income or status based on personal merit. Yet our homes should achieve a certain appear-ance—as television programs teach us to decorate. Changing the appearances of our bodies can be achieved by the multiple products and surgeries available. Many urban areas are finding ways to change their appearances by making homeless people and panhandlers dis-appear from public places. One triumph of American business has been to convince most of us that appearances are the same as or more important than realities. The truth is that some people may appear to be in an upper class because they can afford the trappings, but these present false pictures. Americans who have somehow acquired a great deal of money but will never be considered members of a higher class are numerous, beginning with many sports and entertainment figures. Social class requires that a person claiming membership has ownership of the cultural tenets and practices of a given group.

Sociologist Stanley Aronowitz defines how class works: "*Upper middle class*, for example, is as much a cultural designation as it is economic: it goes with certain neighborhoods and styles of life, including tastes in clothing, entertainment, and choices of secondary and higher education institutions."[5] However, Aronowitz demonstrates that class formation is changing for many reasons: globalization; ongoing migration patterns across borders; the patterns of moving throughout life; groups of jobless people; the speed and development of technology; reduction of benefits, such as pensions; and shifts in governments. But such a complex view of social class is not what attracts African Americans to become members of prosperity churches. The simple statement of the woman in Thompson's church that she was hurting when she first went there stands out as a motivation. The statement of the woman in Dollar's church who wanted her baby to learn to be an entrepreneur in Dollar's preschool gives an idea of what it means to get money, with its hopes for a child's future. The many anecdotes from Rev. Ike's money booklet indicate how money makes people happy.

The desire to wrap oneself in God-given caviar dreams is discussed by Milmon Harrison:

> The people who are [Word of Faith] followers are primarily those whose experience has produced the *desire* for, if not the actualization of, upward socioeconomic mobility . . . using religious doctrine to symbolically and supernaturally level the playing field with respect to access to society's resources. . . . There is tacit acknowledgement of the socially constructed nature of systematic inequality and social structure, but the doctrine teaches that faith in God renders those structures powerless to hinder the divinely appointed upward mobility of the believer.[6]

Prosperity preaching ties Christianity itself to the accumulation of wealth. Prosperity theologies exemplify the use of religion for personal—not communal—gain. Religion then becomes a tool for self-gratification and self-righteousness. A new trinity is created: self, self-interest, and money.

By buying into individualism, this preaching cannot stand in solidarity with the poor—a Christian, after all, should have a prosperity mind set; therefore, a poor person is merely an inconvenience who does not yet know the blessings of God. In spite of the number of poor black people in this economy at this time in history throughout the African diaspora, the "gimme" attitude is built into these religions. As Leroy Thompson said, "I will not be responsible for no broke person."

Because these religions define success by the number of dollars or things a person can grab, a wholehearted support of the status quo and an unquestioned acceptance of the American economic system are given flesh. Yet, there is a certain angry edge that underlies these theologies. bell hooks refers to this in terms of the rage of affluent black people, giving clues to a resulting spiritual sickness. hooks writes: "Affluent blacks are rarely linking their rage to any progressive challenge and critique of white supremacy rooted in solidarity with the black masses. . . . They simply want equal access to privilege within the existing structure."[7]

This sense of getting-something-through-church extends beyond money, as different definitions of prosperity indicate. The personal stories of Johnnie Colemon and Barbara King stand as a kind of proof that health can be achieved with the right mindset. These women's stories of being healed become part and parcel of the mythic lore of the religion.

The expectation that God will deliver as commanded becomes part of the expectation drifting out the doors of prosperity churches to influence other black congregations. It is not unusual for a black pastor to complain that the "sisters in the church want me to pray for them to get husbands!"

Physical ability is another way of structuring a kind of class in some, though not all, prosperity churches. Those people missing from Dollar's church, for example, were the infirm elderly, the mentally ill, and the uncomfortably disabled. Those with a broken but will-be-healed limb are around—they are the "good" disabled;

those with blindness and hearing loss are still "good" because they can earn incomes. But those with so-called disabilities such as congenital Down syndrome were absent. This was brought to mind after I attended another church where a young man with Down syndrome served the community as a greeter. I realized that many black churches are havens for all black people, not just those who are able bodied and able to explain their existence and income as "blessed."

If there is a hazy understanding of social class among Americans, there is a great deal more sophistication about money itself, like teaching young children to be entrepreneurs. When I attended Reverend Ike's Harlem church, it was announced that the following Sunday there would be no service as such but a day-long workshop on buying real estate. These practical lessons do offer black Americans some information about business and money, but connecting them with religious services is subject to abuse. This is reflected by an alert printed in Rev. Ike's order of service: "Many members and friends of our Church have found themselves involved in unscrupulous business schemes. Rev. Ike is asking you to check with him if anyone should approach you in the Church with a business deal. Do not wait until you get involved before you ask for advice. Check before you act! Remember, Christ Community United Church does not sponsor nor endorse individual entrepreneurs."

The importance of money is reflected in the patterns of taking up collections in most prosperity-driven churches. Most notably in the Word of Faith lines, collection is an art. After the sermonizing about first fruiting and tithing to get rich, collections begin. Dollar's church envelope allows the contributor the following selections: tithe, offering, television, building fund, children's ministry, youth ministry, pastor appreciation, the elementary academy, or other; checks, cash, and credit card numbers are gladly accepted. Thompson's envelope has a similar selection for offerings, including a warning label: "We sincerely appreciate your financial support. However, the Board of Directors reserves the right to redirect all funds to the area of the ministry most needed."

These groups' approaches to class and money, while seeming to address black folks' longing for social acceptance, are constructive of brave new black worlds. In a similar construction pattern, gender roles are used as another set of bases for black social acceptance in the Word of Faith churches.

GENDER IN CHURCH

In the Word of Faith lineage, prosperity is tied to "rightness," and the right way to live in America is to fully conform to Victorian-era concepts of how women and men are supposed to act. Such appropriate action is set out as a sign of alignment with God's will. Preaching is used to construct gender roles in ways that privilege men at the expense of women. A prayer by Taffi Dollar directs women on how to converse with God: "Help me to remember that submission is for my protection. I repent where I have not been willing to submit. When I repent, You are faithful and just to forgive me and to cleanse me of all unrighteousness."[8] The development of these ideas in black communities is seen as supporting black men's patriarchal privilege, which is the result of oppression and black women's matriarchal tendencies. The submission of black women to black men gets defined as a way to save the entire, misguided, matriarchal race.

This kind of argument has long created tensions in black communities. Theologian Kelly Brown Douglas situates this ongoing problem.

> There is trouble between men and women. While individuals may enjoy healthy, mutual relationships of respect, the Black community remains plagued by antagonism between the sexes. . . . Open dialogue concerning gender relations is a necessary first step in ameliorating this tension. . . . To confront the issue of strained male/female relationships in the Black community would mean acknowledging the presence of sexism. . . . Even more daunting for many in the Black community is the fact that a serious confrontation with sexism implies the even more difficult discussion of Black sexuality.[9]

Womanist ethicist Toinette Eugene described principles for embodied relationships that can counter negative social structures. One of her principles states: "[I]t is in the context of black relationships formed and affirmed in the black family, the black community and the black Church, running counter to the culture of despair, where we find the convergence of race, gender, and sexuality that guides us with our past and calls us into the future of justice and sustained hope."[10] Here is a very different view from Dollar's "virtuous" woman. Eugene might agree with how relationships between men and women can be a prayerful experience, but the submissiveness of the woman at all times, for her own good, does not set up a system of countering a culture of despair. There is need for open discussions about gender roles in black communities. There is need for more frank discussion of gender and sexuality and sexism in black churches. Taffi Dollar's male-dominated views are more than a form of denying gender inequities; the tenet of the submissive virtuous woman becomes a construction of oppression, barring constructive dialogue between black women and men. Such prosperity preaching ultimately damages relationships between women and men, in families and in communities.

There is one other way that gendered structures are seen as the men (Dollar, Ike, and Thompson) build dynasties—but King and Colemon do not seem to have done so. Just to be clear, what the men have done in setting up family businesses is not unique to Word of Faith line churches, but can be found all over black communities. The pastor's wife or first lady and the preacher's kids in many a black church hold status among the members and sometime become mini-despots. Is this dynastic tendency an indication of how black church identifies itself, as patriarch led and run? Is this the way that church members can identify their religious connection? In light of megachurches, does the dynasty represent a transference of the sense of being a religious community ("When we see *them*, we know who *we* are")? Is there fear of the end of a ministry or church if the family does not safeguard it? Many a black church has begun at the hands of an inspirational leader, and the vision has continued and grown through the membership. What do these kinds of ecclesiastic structures mean for and in the twenty-first century? These questions cannot be answered here, and longer discussions are needed. But it has been interesting to see how some prosperity preachers have adopted this black culture-derived patriarchal system and blessed it with another set of Bibles.

CREATING PROSPEROUS BLACK SOCIETIES

I visited Word of Faith International Center in Southfield, Michigan, the home church of Keith Butler. The church is composed of several buildings on several acres, a former monastery that has been renovated. Butler's political ties are well-known throughout the community and overlap into his church's life, especially as he has run for state office representing black Republican life.

On the day I was there, Keith Butler was not physically present, but his presence was well-established. The photos of the ministerial staff are displayed in the foyer. Among these, Bishop Butler and his pastor wife (who directs the Women of Virtue fellowship) smile next to their two children. His son, Keith II, is listed as "co-pastor." He is married, his wife assisting in their ministry in another church in Oklahoma, also focusing on the Women of Virtue. The majority of these ministers have attended the Rhema Bible institute (Kenneth Hagin's center), through which they were ordained. The other photos showed men and women, some of whom had the Butler surname. The younger ministry staff photos set a conservative tone, the people were garbed in dresses, suits, and ties, but no trendy clothes were in evidence among ministers or other young people there.

I attended on a "youth" Sunday, and the twenty-ish generation had taken over the church. But the messages followed the established household codes, ensuring that there would be black prosperous men and virtuous women for the son's future ministry position. With the growth of this twenty-something ministry group, the shaping of a new generation was clearly taking place, a generation for whom this theology would be the primary formation in their lives.

The structure of the service reflected the youth focus. Young people were playing instruments, even though the paid professionals were still in evidence. The forty-or-so-voice choir was composed of mostly young people. One part of the service featured bringing forward those who were about to get married, affirming the sanctity of marriage and the nuclear family before the community.

The shaping of the young community was clear in the sermon of Keith Jr. He began with a biblical quotation from John: abide in belief and you shall know the truth and the truth shall set you free. He defined truth as the Word bringing freedom from "level one and level two" sins. He went on to cite "Brother" Hagin's definition of "fake curse words," a euphemism for euphemisms: the words everybody knows the meaning for, and that are, therefore, really the same as curse words. Fake curse words are level one sins.

Level two sins are the ones of the "filthy flesh," taking a new direction from the instructions in Colossians 3 for believers to "mortify" their flesh. Mortifying flesh does not mean that Christians are to suffer, but that they are to willingly forego association with those level two sins. Keith Jr. then proceeded to explain through his own experience how sins were to be avoided. His wife had given birth and he then had to suffer through six weeks of celibacy. He was careful not to look at other women. For instance, he saw a beautiful woman in the mall and because he had been celibate he had to look away or, as he instructed men, "bounce your eyes." This "bouncing" is to avoid committing adultery, which a man does who lusts in his heart. He stated proudly that he loves his new daughter—but waiting (while his wife healed) was so hard for him. "And it's not possible to just have a little. That's what the flesh says when you are on a diet, you can have just a little taste. You can't really have a little taste because you will just go back for more." His definition of his "suffering" through celibacy exhibits a level of narcissism. But for Butler, as a result of being a believer and knowing the Truth, he is set free: "We live sin-free lives." Even as he assists in constructing a brave new congregation for the future through his sermon, what is occurring at the same time is the construction and refinement of their version of the Word of Faith theology. Any religion's theology must continue to develop over generations; Keith Jr. is part of process of clarifying that aspect of the future.

SOCIAL POWER OF THE BLACK PROSPERITY PREACHING

No matter what critiques might be offered about prosperity preaching in black communities, the creative uses of religion by African Americans to address questions and seek answers must be recognized. Contemporary preachers draw from multiple sources to address a black spirituality of longing. Daddy Grace, James Forman, and others brought their own sense of creativity in developing black religious thought. These are often ignored or dismissed. To truly understand African American intellectual history, creative dynamics in constructing religious expression must be taken into account.

Prosperity preaching in black communities is part of larger trends reshaping black identities. Continued desire to be more fully accepted into the United States' social structures along with greater American consumerism is leading to other dynamics in black communal life. Publicized successes of a few black people add fuel to the desire, encompassing new identities expressed in religious language. But there is a significant difference between being self-serving and seeking self-preservation. Such distinction is not clear in prosperity preaching. Are these new black identities less committed to justice, less interested in the idea of a racial unity, uninterested in ideas of black community building? Has the desire to totally escape from poor black ghetto life limited our ability to re-imagine black community life and meaning?

The full meaning of these changes is only beginning to be seen. And often the changes in black social structures throw levels of confusion into the traditional black church, as described by African American religious historian Gayraud Wilmore.

> In my day we were either Baptist, Methodist, or Pentecostal. . . . We were all essentially orthodox in our theology—generally following white neoorthodox or "evangelical" theologians and conservative Christian educators. Our congregations were more mixed than they are today in the sense that the poor, the middle class, and the wealthy sat side by side in the pews. . . . Today, looking down from the pulpit on a Sunday morning, you don't know what you have out there. Clearly not many are poor and oppressed in the ordinary sense. The young people are gone. You really don't know what people believe, if they believe anything. . . . Among the congregation, you can find agnostics, practical atheists, younger members on the verge of going over to Islam, yoga practitioners . . . adherents of various TV and radio evangelists . . . and folks who are proverbially at sea—drifting to and fro among a variety of operative worldviews.[11]

The social changes impacting understandings of how black people identify themselves also are central to the theological changes that result from prosperity preaching.

8 | PROSPERITY, BLACK LIBERATION, AND THEOLOGIES

his final chapter brings us to the theological analysis of prosperity preaching in black communities. What is the "good news" of theologies of prosperity? Might it align with the gospel preached in other black churches? As a theologian, my first inclination in analysis of prosperity theologies is to put them in dialogue with basic Christian theology. But this book has been focused on this preaching in the greater black community, not just as isolated types. To continue in this vein, any analysis of prosperity theologies in black communities should not become separated from the real lives of African Americans. Therefore I begin with a cautionary tale from a friend who is a member of Eddie Long's church in Atlanta.

Rita, for the past few years, has been a job readiness counselor. "Job readiness" is a category that grew after welfare policy changed and people could no longer receive public assistance payments without demonstrating that they were actively seeking employment. The requirements to receive assistance have become stringent, and there is a time limit during which a person can receive welfare. Rita has stepped into an agency's position where she can be of assistance to the mostly black clientele. One morning, a black woman client announced that she was going on a job interview. Rita saw that the woman was inappropriately dressed: she was large, wearing a t-shirt with no bra and leggings with run-over sport shoes. Rita took her to the clothes closet on site and worked to help the woman get dressed, finding a bra and business attire. As they talked during the process of picking out clothes, Rita tried to make a point about dressing for work, asking the woman, "Well, how do people on your street dress when they go to work?" To which the woman replied: "Nobody works on my street."

For Rita, churches like Long's are "changing the mindsets of our people. We've got the generational thing in terms of welfare. But that is not our history; we used to be entrepreneurs. I remember how my grandfather used to make money with his own business. Today we need to be empowered to get back to that level of self-sufficiency. If it takes the church, the center of black people's lives, to get them to think outside the box they're in, then why not? Reverend Long gave a sermon about where our dreams are today, have we lost them? And we need this. Do whatever we can to change black people's mindsets."

Rita's comments help to situate the following theological discussion. The need of which she speaks is not just for a poor black woman who lives on a block where few engage in regular wage labor. It is also a need for upwardly striving black folks who are learning how to navigate the social world outside ghetto realities. It is a need for the black middle class who often have great debt, low savings, and little equity in homes, yet without the social capital of a well-established network to cushion them should their jobs evaporate. It is not just the theories about theology, but real people's lives that are involved, and this comes back to the spirituality of longing, ideas to which I will return throughout the chapter.

THE THEOLOGICAL SHAPE OF PROSPERITY

From the exploration of the preceding chapters, it is clear that Word of Faith churches have a different operative theology from the Unity or Science of Religion grouping. In both theological frames, there are ranges of religious expression possible, as the extreme expressions of Rev. Ike demonstrate. In spite of the differences, there are some general theological principles operating. Two major categories of import for theologies of prosperity are evil/sin and God.

The category of sin or evil is defined differently from that traditionally preached in black Christian churches. In some ways, the prosperity approach is less defined, limited to how an individual person is thinking, and how his or her life is expressed through demonstrated prosperity. Of course, prosperity is defined differently across the range of these theologies, from the broad-spectrum idea of "all the good things given" by the Creator to the very specific signals of being "blessed" by money and material things. Systemic evil and social sin practically disappear in these views, becoming things to ignore as the individual lives into God's promises.

For the Unity/Science of Religion groupings, incidents of sin are not completely ignored but dealt with as issues that must be forgiven if the person is to move on to the next level of life. This is forgiveness that begins with the person forgiving her- or himself for being in or affected by a given situation. After forgiving self and any others involved, the mind is used to create the new situation that is desired rather than dwelling on the sinful part of experience.

For Word of Faith, sin is a "them" rather than "us" experience. As Keith Butler Jr. explained in his sermon, there are level one and level two sins, the worst of which are "fleshly" and both of which are signs of human weakness. That human weakness is also reflected in the "sin" of poverty, because a person is not living as God wishes: in truth. That truth is expressed in a person's life by tithing, which seems to be the answer to all evil in this religion. The tithe is given to Jesus, Creflo Dollar states, not to "some man. The preacher may be the one collecting the tithes, but you have placed your dedicated thing before the throne of God. If someone chooses to do something stupid with your tithe after you've presented it, that's between that man and God."[1] The implications of this understanding of sin are explained as Dollar describes how to avoid a miscarriage.

> If you are one of those women who get pregnant only to lose your baby, there are several things you need to examine in your life. First of all, are you and your husband tithing? Secondly, check to see if there is strife in your household, and, thirdly, check out any biological issues that may be causing you to miscarry. In fact, you can take your tithe and sow that tithe and say, "In the name of Jesus, I have a right to the fruit of my body. Now, I rebuke whatever is going on here, and in the name of Jesus, I line my life up with the Word of God.[2]

The Unity/Religious Science or Word of Faith version brings a decidedly capitalistic twist to the conversation since, seemingly, a black spirituality of longing can be filled by a God who grants gifts of cash.

These views may be helpful, as Rita points out, challenging the individual person to become empowered, despite history, with a mindset that doing otherwise is sinfulness. The rejection of personal and social limits, especially sin, would have great meaning for black Americans who have yet to recover from a long, brutal history. The motivation to avoid sin and pull oneself up by the spiritual bootstraps has pastoral implications, inviting people to will or think themselves to a demonstrated, material salvation. However, this theological view is not new. Indeed, it resonates with a fifth-century heresy, Pelagianism, that has made regular appearances over the centuries. The original heresy focused on the importance of the human will to achieve salvation. In Pelagianism, the role of God is limited to a grace-dispensing function, available anytime the person chooses to take it. Pelagius was a monk who originated the ideas sixteen hundred years ago, not as heretical thought, but for pastoral reasons as he tried to answer the longings of his congregation.

Like their Pelagian forerunner, both the Unity/Religious Science and Word of Faith versions of sin are intimately related to contemporary versions of limited views of God. Johnnie Colemon's stirring sermon about the power of God who is fully able to do all things would seem to reflect Christian scripture. But this "God-in-me" individual is invited to think of I AM (God) as a personal reflection. The individual person's will controls God/self. In Word of Faith theology, God is expected to perform to human qualifications, filling all of the believer's needs on demand. For all the expressions of these prosperity religions, the language of "contract" and covenant and Law are constantly used when talking about human relationships with God: *I* enter a contract for certain goods and services, they are delivered according to the agreed upon schedule. But can humans really set the schedule? How much negotiation can *I* enter into with God?

At the same time, another reason some black Americans might be attracted to these religions is that the theologies, especially the idea of mind and will control, may resonate with cultural understandings of religion by recalling African conceptualizations of the holistic connections between all things. As an example, the hoodoo doctor or root worker believes in using knowledge and intention to control aspects of life. Rev. Ike's sale of blessed prayer cloths to assist in "uncrossing" jinxed situations is directly in line with the hoodoo doctor's traditions. This mixture of a religion's ideas with black cultural ideas is not unique to the prosperity preaching's growth. Black religious creativity is part of the intellectual tradition of this people.

Such creativity has aided in unique development of certain aspects of Christian thought, including the historic birth of the black church from the hollers and ring shouts of enslaved Africans. In general, African American religious creativity is a wonder that has helped build sustaining communities and has helped to retain cultural perspectives. But that same creativity is a two-edged sword that can construct new problems, as blending ideas to meet real needs may not assist with personal growth. For instance, a religion constructed for one's physical comfort ultimately does not assist spiritual maturity, even if it addresses a spirituality of longing. Neither does a pushover Deity represent a mature view of God. When I was five, I thought God would be just like my grandmother because she let me do anything that I wanted. Had I retained this view into adulthood, serious spiritual problems would be indicated. Human beings should grow in wisdom and grace. That growth happens when each person and community expect that spiritualities (understood as a defined way of being in the world) will mature. That growth implies that religious people learn other ways to develop mature relationships with God. But a convenient Deity does not assist this growth and, in the prosperity tradition, turns God into a magic ATM machine.

Prosperity religions generally develop a theology of here-and-now. The leaders do not draw from centuries of theological development, but the decades of their religions' existence. I found that the ideas in these churches were reduced and simplified into easily digestible concepts so that people had immediate use of a pain-free religious experience. However, what does it mean to be a religious person? Today, with the variety of religious practices and social concepts available to black people through education, technology, and television, there is no simple category of "us" to be found, if there ever was. My friend Rita wants some black Americans to relearn the power of dreams, and she views the black church as an appropriate vehicle for delivering dreams. But there is more to a faith life than satisfying personal dreams. Sometimes, faith experiences challenge the believer to be better, to accept ethical "oughts" even though self-ishness would dictate another, easier choice.

This dilemma points out the complexity of the concept of faith. Faith cannot be reduced to simple platitudes, even if the platitude is taken from a biblical passage. Faith encompasses the belief, action, and trust of individual people as well as the person's communities of family, neighborhood, and congregation. All of these aspects shape persons' and communities' faith lives. These same aspects of faith— belief, action, and trust—also grow over a person's lifetime, so that a twelve-year-old will not have the same understanding of faith as does a fifty-year-old. Each person and community should grow and mature into a healthy spirituality. These ideas lead to a consideration of how theological constructions are involved in and part of the life of a religious community.

THEOLOGY CONSTRUCTED IN COMMUNITY

Theologies are constructed over time: the initial ideas about faith are shaped in community dialogues. These dialogues happen as leaders shape churches, as members respond, while the wider society changes. Theologies of prosperity reflect all these changes, altering yet again when black communities interact with them. Rev. Ike's early writing, from a more solidly Religious Science perspective, is different from his later sales of prayers cloths. Usually, though, one part of a theology grows out of the religious community, which accepts or rejects the new thinking, just as Pelagianism had been rejected. I am greatly oversimplifying the complex processes involved in theological development to make several points.

The earlier prosperity thought of Father Divine or Daddy Grace, of Forman or Garvey, may reflect developments from within black communities. Yet, the importing of newer forms, particularly from the Word of Faith lineage, has less a sense of organic growth from within the black community than becoming part of existing systems. For instance, was Taffi Dollar's prayer for Vice President Dick Cheney really in the black community's best interests? Was this prayer a response to the community's need or was another agenda at work? How would support of Dick Cheney bring "God into the government" as Dollar prayed? Asking and answering these kinds of questions in a religion's community sharpens the theological constructions. Otherwise, a new kind of colonization-by-religion occurs.

Some of that sharpening of theology happens as leaders of the religious community enter dialogues with other leaders. The Association for Global New Thought mentioned in chapter 6 is developing a clearer identity and, in the process, sharper theological statements.

Theological developments with prosperity themes are not separate from the larger community of the black church. Other black theologians have made strong statements about prosperity thinking, including James Cone. Cone stated, "You don't realize you can be very successful institutionally and also a failure in terms of the mission that called you into being. When you talk about the cross you are talking about the focus on the little ones, the ones who are hurting, suffering, who don't have a voice. Churches are reaching out to middle-class people." Other black pastors have comments as well, as did Jeremiah Wright, pastor of Trinity United Church of Christ in Chicago. "What are you doing about why there is hunger? What are you doing to change the laws? You've got kids who cannot read. What are you doing about that? Have another worship service?"[3]

These kinds of deliberations have some impact on the development of theologies of prosperity, as evidenced in Baptist Eddie Long's adoption of such ideas. Or it may be that black prosperity churches circle the wagons more tightly, keeping out the ideas of the Cones or Wrights. Or new forms may develop, such as Prophecology. To be community does not mean uniformity or even agreement. The role of community is not to merely restrict the freedom of religious believers. Instead, community becomes a sounding board for the ideas that come while living faithful lives; clarity is always needed. Seminaries are part of the conversations, again working to sharpen theological statements.

But resistance to participation in these larger conversations by taking anti-intellectual stances, as do most Word of Faith churches, is counterproductive to the development of theology. Any Christian who believes that God created him or her would have to admit that human intelligence was also created. On theoretical levels, misusing or ignoring the intellect is to ultimately abuse the gift of the Creator, denying God's divinity and authority. On some very practical levels, trying to construct a theology without using the full gift of human intellect results in the twisted kind of sermon that Keith Butler Jr. delivered.

Theological development within prosperity churches is also dependent on forms of dialogue. Johnnie Colemon's break with the Unity Association must have had an impact, especially since she began her own successful organization. But do the successes of these prosperity churches inhibit theological dialogue? When people are involved in a successful enterprise, is there a greater tendency, as in Enron's glory days, to avoid critiquing what seems to be working? Does analysis only begin when there is failure, as in Delores's experiences with a preacher's ineffectual attempt to use prosperity theology?

But another situation in the development of prosperity theologies has a direct impact on black church. The concept of black church, returning to Barbara Holmes' definition, is a meta-actual reality, that is, unlimited by a physical space. Under the oppressive conditions that forced black Americans to create alternate social structures, a theologically shaped church occurred. If African Americans had never known oppressions, never experienced segregation, and had been able to be accepted in the nation, this black church would not have developed as it did. Those components helped to shape the theological grounding of the black church. Black church communities never marched in lock step; diversity existed within each regional group of African Americans. However, there were some links between people, some sense that recalled the African proverb that sticks bound together are more difficult to break.

Now, with the prosperity preachers' emphases on what members can individually obtain, community can easily be translated into a sole concern with personal problems and needs. The individual becomes more important than the group and, therefore, the individualism of American society replaces active concerns for social justice. Some prosperity preachers' focus on controlling the mind as a way to control negative aspects of reality also alters group dynamics within black communities. Self-esteem is a good thing for black minds. Yet when the individual "self" is an exclusive focus, religion becomes a set of exercises in narcissism.

The meaning of religious community also changes as prosperity churches significantly use multiple technologies. Television and the Internet may have benefits for keeping members in touch with each other, especially those who have physical difficulty traveling. But for more people, the use of these technologies becomes substitutes for actually being in community. Community via a machine that can be stopped and started is not the same as being in touch with other human beings.

The websites of many of the prosperity churches, along with the audio and video compact discs, are well produced and of studio quality. Do the studio-enhanced sounds, brush-stroked pictures, and edited worship services really constitute a religious community? Or are false images addicting, becoming points of reference against which real-time church services are always measured? If theology is defined through interactions, what kind of theology occurs through online worship? In spite of the technological advances of television, iPods, Internet, chat rooms, and blackberries, the building of community still happens slowly, person by person. Growing in wisdom involves learning to be part of the human world, which is not always perfect and controllable. Prosperity preaching brings a privatized religion that moves away from the importance of the communal base to an imbalanced valuing of the individual. Spiritual and emotional growth depends on human contact.

BLACK LIBERATION AND RELIGION

Attempting to answer black folks' spirituality of longing did not begin with prosperity churches. Such conversations have been occurring within the black religious community all along. Among black religion scholars, the questions regarding poverty and oppression took on heightened importance as civil rights, the ending of legal segregation, and new social unrest grew from the late

1950s. Beginning in the late 1960s, James Cone began the development of a black theology of liberation, answering challenges to the efficacy of religion raised through the black power movement. The development of that theological stream has widened throughout black religious scholarship. In the 1980s, black women cultivated their distinct ethical and theological streams, related to both black liberation and feminist thought, and used the term womanist to describe their work. While ideas from several of these thinkers have been incorporated throughout this book, a more focused discussion will enhance the investigation of prosperity preaching in black communities.

Womanist theologian Kelly Brown Douglas discusses part of the problem with contemporary Christianity as coming from the historic construction of a platonized tradition. By platonized, she refers to Greek philosophy's view of the human person: "The Platonic belief in the world of forms (that is, the immaterial/true world) as being different *and* superior to the world of senses (that is the material/earthly world) combined in Christian thought with the Stoic ethic defined by *apatheia* [ascetic control of the sensual appetites]."[4] The preference for the spiritual (immaterial) over the earthly (physical) was extended in Western European theological constructions so as to demonize black bodies, culture, and spirituality. But black Christianity's distinctive character becomes clear during times of great oppression, when it is "liable to nurture a revolutionary/nationalist spirit. . . . In effect, Black faith in the justice of God makes clear that God affirms the sacred value of the Black body."[5] Douglas contends that black Americans of faith reflect ambivalence toward their own bodies and experiences, adopting this platonized view of their own beings.

While Douglas focuses on how black Americans fall into negative views of their own sexuality as a problem, I extend her argument here. Prosperity forms of Christianity remains true to a platonized view by turning the material into demonstrations of the spiritual. The ambivalence in black expressions of platonized Christianity are expressed in some prosperity religions by setting black Americans into rejections of other aspects of their blackness, including cultural expressions and community support. The rejection of community and the subsequent narrow focus on the self is another indication of a platonized view, one that denies the importance of race and unquestioningly adopts individualistic, spiritualized mindsets. There is a dimension of self-hatred expressed. It was expressed in Leroy Thompson's church when he told the members he'd have to hurt them to help them. It was expressed in Creflo Dollar's church as Taffi Dollar prayed for Dick Cheney. Or when Creflo was pushing tickets to a church event and jokingly warned the congregation that nobody should approach him during the event with any problems, because he'd be there to have fun. People may defend these incidents as "just kidding," but there are more serious beliefs indicated. Black self-hatred in a headlong plunge to grasping materialism is shown in the book title "*Why Should White Guys Have All the Fun?*" Rita's comments that black people need to dream again and change mindsets are important, but doing so will not necessarily be a fun task. The difficulties involved in creating positive change is witnessed in the work of black and womanist theologians.

Theologian Dwight Hopkins puts issues of poverty and black life into context:

> In the American civic fabric, there inheres an unspoken prerequisite for success: the requirement of whiteness. Power and wealth ownership reside in white hands. This contradicts the purpose of theological anthropology [relationship with God and peaceful community life]. . . . Nevertheless, God has called human beings to continue the struggle toward the original created understanding of what it meant to be a full human being.[6]

But, Hopkins says, there is a strong tradition within African American religious life in which "God tabernacles especially among the African American poor and affirms [their] positive cultural and political traditions and practices."[7] Black Americans choose which path to take: that which accepts the (white) premise of how to be successful, or that coming from their own communities' values.

To escape this quandary will require some new thinking. Emilie Townes is a womanist ethicist who gives an indication of a new direction. Her words are reflective of both Hopkins' theological anthropology and Douglas's platonized Christian thought:

These hierarchies of age, class, gender, sexual orientation, race, and on and on are held in place by violence, fear, ignorance, acquiescence. The endgame is to win and win it all—status, influence, place, creation. Our world needs a new (or perhaps ancient) vision molded by justice and peace rather than winning or loosing if we are to unhinge the cultural production of evil.[8]

Prosperity religions bring all these issues into tension in very critical ways. Other concerns flow from the ideas of Christian platonized theology, theological anthropology, and the need for a new vision.

Womanist theologian Delores Williams invites reflection on the meanings of salvation in social contexts. "Womanists and Black male liberation theologians . . . can provide ideas about salvation in a social context for Black Christians who want to understand how Black people can be saved in the material world."[9] More than simply economic analyses, connections between ideas about money and material things and religion need new greater attention. It is not a simple "us" or "them" question but one that warrants much deeper exploration. What does it mean for black folks to be saved in this world? What are religious responses for the right use of money? How can black communal faith life be enriched and what does money mean in that context? What *is* church?

Williams also states that destruction of black communities by white hate groups should be addressed as part of salvation. "Today Black people seek salvation for the African American communities whose major institution—the Black church—is threatened in some areas of the country with destruction by members of White hate groups."[10] Prosperity preaching offers new forms of hatred within black communities, as puppets of white pastors and government officials offer advice about what African Americans should do to get ahead in this society. This is very disturbing, as black church members, in the theology of prosperity driven churches, become replicas of the very people who bring death into our communities.

Beyond these ideas, Williams calls for an examined faith:

> An examined faith is a critical way of seeing that shows those things in a belief system that are life-threatening and life-taking. An examined faith inspires people to discard beliefs, images, and

symbols that have the potential to support scapegoating and destruction. . . . An examined faith discards any religion and any God who commands Black people to sit idly contemplating love of their oppressors while they (Black people) are threatened and destroyed by those who hate them.[11]

When people come to churches, although they do not have the language of the theologians, they ask the same questions from the heart of their longing: "Why are black people mistreated? Why are we poor? What can I do to help myself and my family? What does America mean for black people? How can Christianity help me out of these dilemmas?" Historically, some answers were developed under the leadership of Garvey and Forman. Today, besides the prosperity angle, some black churches have connected with members' African heritage, offering trips and festivals that celebrate Africans across the Diaspora. Other churches have significant social programs and dare to respond to any question that comes before the community, whether it's the AIDS epidemic among African Americans and its methods of transmission or the issues of gender roles and sex education. Some churches are not afraid to educate their congregations not only about social problems, but they present a full explanation of the basis of their denomination's theology. The leadership in some churches is not afraid to accept the gifts of members' talents, whether in finances or in counseling, in order to strengthen the whole community. But these answers may still not have the central focus that sets up the answer to the black spirituality of longing.

Critical to these discussions is a return to the aspect of black church life that Obery Hendricks refers to as the prophetic imperative. The core of prophecy is truth-telling, especially important because the Christian gospel is radical; it is not political conservatism. To be prophetic, Christians must beware of becoming "bibliolaters" who worship the Bible without historical context or study. Being prophetic also means reclaiming a tradition of "interiority," or moments of meditation within worship services.[12] These ideas constitue more than just denouncing aspects of prosperity theology. People need to find answers in their religious experiences. To achieve such honesty is not an easy task; there are no quick fixes. To focus on truth telling could answer the spirituality of longing, but not indulge and pander to it.

IN CONCLUSION

This book has not said all there is to say about prosperity preaching in black communities. We have looked at some aspects of black church history and its development, as well as new growth through black and womanist theologies. We have considered interactions between African Americans, sociocultural shifts, and economic issues. The desire for money can be seen as being a way out of social rejection concurrent with black people's desire for a relevant church home. Prosperity preaching has gathered these desires, even as it disrupted the fabric of the black community, evidenced by the controversy at Interdenominational Theological Center's graduation.

I have advocated understanding the complexities involved in the growth of these new religious expressions. The knowledge should include recognition of the differences between the types of prosperity preaching. Further, as a spirituality of longing is made more explicit, the many layers of economic and national issues may be addressed in new ways. Black cultural styles of leadership and communication have been critical as new theologies—such as Word of Faith or Religious Science—are imported into the communities. However, the uses of these prosperity religions do not really bring an end to the culture of despair; there is a certain cynicism toward African Americans in the pastoral applications of prosperity, using their own cultural views against them. These gospels of materiality, though, indicate the depth at which the longings in black communities have yet to be addressed. Stepping back from the prosperity religions for a moment, let us look at other options.

If black folks have any wisdom from our accumulated experiences in America, how might the lures of a culture of despair be countered? One way to think about the options is offered by a pastor, Otis Moss, who sees three main strands of theology in the black church today. One is a "pimp theology" that is based on the question "What can you do for me?" The second is a theology that prostitutes the gospel, asking, "What can I do for you?" Finally, prophetic theology asks, "What can we do together?"[13] Following Moss's line of thought, prophetic theology must be grounded in community.

At the same time, womanist and black theologians continue to analyze economic realities in light of faith. The need to actively work against white hatred while living an examined faith, as Delores Williams charges, is particularly difficult to accomplish in a time when American society tries to deny race's importance and racism's significance. One route into living an examined faith is by analyzing what it means to be privileged in black communities. So what defines affluence for African Americans? What responsibilities are accrued to those who are the haves or the have-nots? What kind of dreams can be held in common that will bridge economic gaps? In order to become agents who actually counter despair and find concrete solutions, it will continue to be imperative to analyze changing social structures. To counter the culture of despair there is additional need to recognize how religion can be used to aid spiritual maturity in black communities while feeding hope. As part of that analysis, it is more important than ever for womanists and black theologians and ethicists to actively present deeper economic analyses.

Black culture is recognized and held as valuable in order to utilize the holistic perspectives that are built in. This appreciation of culture should be done consciously and carefully, not by singing a few gospel tunes or draping kente cloth over altars. Garvey's African Orthodox Church and even Father Divine's kingdom banquets came from black cultural perspectives, taking history and identity into account, to build something that could answer people's needs. Their work contrasts with that of prosperity preachers.

Part of what the prosperity preachers do for black folks is put on a show that exudes wealth and glamour, not just at church but all the time. When Atlanta pastor Barbara King was married a few years ago, the invitations to her wedding were the hottest ticket in town. Social acceptance is seen as happening symbolically for all black Americans as King is selected as one of the First Ladies of Faith for a makeup line. These symbols of social success and acceptance become the center of prosperity teaching, identifying a new heart of their gospel. In doing so, black American religious life becomes even more a marketed commodity.

The overlapping concerns from African Americans' political and social lives helped bring prosperity thinking to the fore. These concerns are made more complex by black spirituality and values. The dilemmas raised in black communities by prosperity thinking are numerous, as I have described; resolving the dilemmas will take time and concentrated efforts.

There is, however, one significant hope for all that has occurred as a result of the changes in black socioreligious life. Prosperity preaching did spotlight the hopes of black communities for acceptance. It can be a starting place to find out what really should be done to achieve social justice. To define the parameters, I borrow the semantics of prosperity thinking, moving them from a bumper-sticker mentality toward a stronger constructive statement: Naming the history and values of black religious meaning and claiming these benefits to achieve a wholesome life for the wider community can begin now.

CHAPTER 1

1. Barbara A. Holmes, *Joy Unspeakable: Contemplative Practices of the Black Church* (Minneapolis: Fortress Press, 2004), 5.

2. Michael Eric Dyson, *I May Not Get There with You: The True Martin Luther King Jr.* (New York: Free Press, 2000), 134–35.

3. Ibid., 128.

4. Ibid., 127.

5. Claude F. Jacobs, "Rituals of Healing in African American Spiritual Churches," in *Religion and Healing in America*, ed. Linda L. Barnes and Susan S. Sered (New York: Oxford University Press, 2005), 333.

6. Carter G. Woodson, *The History of the Negro Church* (Washington, D.C.: Associated Publishers, 1921), 250.

7. Ibid., 251–52.

8. Ibid., 273.

9. Ibid., 301–02.

10. E. Franklin Frazier, *The Negro Church in America* (New York: Schocken Books, 1974), 10.

11. Ibid., 76.

12. Ibid., 77.

13. Ibid., 58–71.

14. Ibid., 38.

15. Ibid.

16. Ibid., 39.

17. Ibid., 40.

18. One exemplary study that has looked extensively at the ways black church life was used to socialize African Americans into white value systems is Evelyn Brooks Higginbotham, *Righteous Discontent: The Women's Movement in the Black Baptist Church 1880–1920* (Cambridge: Harvard University Press 1993).

19. C. Eric Lincoln, *The Black Church Since Frazier* (New York: Schocken Books, 1974).

20. Ibid., 106.

21. Ibid.

22. Ibid., 124.

23. James H. Cone, *God of the Oppressed* (New York: Seabury Press, 1975), 21.

CHAPTER 2

1. Stephen Steinberg, "The Liberal Retreat from Race During the Post–Civil Rights Era," in *The House That Race Built: Black Americans, U.S. Terrain,* ed. Wahneema Lubiano (New York: Pantheon Books, 1997), 19.

2. Manning Marable, *Living Black History: How Reimagining the African-American Past Can Remake America's Racial Future* (New York: Basic Civitas Books, 2006), 208.

3. Marcellus Andrews, *The Political Economy of Hope and Fear: Capitalism and the Black Condition in America* (New York: New York University Press, 1999), 121.

4. Ibid., 122.

5. Ibid., 148.

6. U.S. Bureau of Labor Statistics, http://www.bls.gov/ces/, accessed December 8, 2006.

7. U.S. Bureau of Labor Statistics, *Occupational Outlook Handbook, 2006–7 Edition,* www.bls.gov/oco December 2006.

8. Marable, *Living Black History,* 215.

9. Economic Research Service, "2006 Farm Income Forecast," www.usda.gov, accessed March 2007.

10. Timothy Pigford et al., Plaintiffs v. Dan Glickman, Secretary, United States Department of Agriculture, Defendant, Civil Action No. 97-1978 PLF, decided April 14, 1999. http://www.ewg.org/reports_content/black farmers/pdf/PigfordOpinion.pdf.

11. Micaela di Leonardo, "White Lies, Black Myths: Rape, Race and the Black 'Underclass'" in *The Gender Sexuality Reader,* ed. Roger N. Lancaster and Micaela di Leonardo (New York: Routledge, 1997), 60.

12. Robert J. Weems Jr., *Desegregating the Dollar: African American Consumerism in the Twentieth Century* (New York: New York University Press 1998), 131.

13. Ann L. Riley, "Health and Self-Esteem Among African Americans," *African American Research Perspectives,* vol. 9, no. 1 (Winter 2003), 158.

14. Reginald Lewis and Blair S. Walker, *"Why Should White Guys Have All the Fun?": How Reginald Lewis Created a Billion Dollar Business Empire* (New York: John Wiley and Sons, 1995).

15. Earl Graves, *How to Succeed in Business without Being White: Straight Talk on Making It in America* (New York: Harper, 1997).

16. Dennis Kimbro and Napoleon Hill, *Think and Grow Rich: A Black Choice* (New York: Ballantine Books, 1997).

17. Cornel West, "Nihilism in Black America" in *Black Popular Culture*, ed. Gina Dent, (Seattle: Bay Press, 1992), 38.

18. National Urban League, *The State of Black America 2005: Prescriptions for Change*, ed. Lee Daniels, 12. Available at http://www.nul.org/thestate ofblackamerica.html.

19. Ibid., 18.

20. Tavis Smiley, *The Covenant with Black America* (Chicago: Third World Press 2006), x.

21. Flora Bridges, *Resurrection Song: African-American Spirituality* (Maryknoll, N.Y.: Orbis Books, 2001), 167.

22. Dwight N. Hopkins, *Being Human: Race, Culture, and Religion* (Minneapolis: Augsburg Fortress, 2005), 13–14.

23. Leslie King-Hammond, "The Bible and the Aesthetics of Sacred Space in Twentieth-Century African American Experience," in *African Americans and the Bible: Sacred Texts and Social Textures*, ed. Vincent L. Wimbush (New York: Continuum, 2001), 433–34.

24. Alice Walker, "Introduction: Sweet Honey in the Rock—The Sound of Our Own Culture," in Bernice Johnson Reagon and Sweet Honey in the Rock, *We Who Believe in Freedom: Sweet Honey in the Rock Still on the Journey* (New York: Anchor Books, 1993), 9.

25. Marable, *Living Black History*, 210.

26. Emilie M. Townes, *Womanist Ethics and the Production of Evil* (New York: Palgrave Macmillan 2006), 45.

27. Marable, *Living Black History*, 63–64.

28. Cècile Coquet, "My God Is a Time-God: How African American Folk Oratory Speaks (of) Time," in *African Americans and the Bible: Sacred Texts and Social Textures*, ed. Vincent Wimbush (New York: Continuum, 2001), 534.

29. Larry Murphy, "Piety and Liberation: A Historical Exploration of African American Religion and Social Justice," in *Blow the Trumpet in Zion: Global Vision and Action for the 21st-century Black Church*, edited by Iva E. Carruthers, Frederick D. Haynes III, and Jeremiah A. Wright Jr. (Minneapolis: Fortress Press 2005), 37.

CHAPTER 3

1. Milmon F. Harrison, *Righteous Riches: The Word of Faith Movement in Contemporary African American Religion* (New York: Oxford University Press 2005), 148–49.

2. Beverly Hall Lawrence, *Reviving the Spirit: A Generation of African Americans Goes Home to Church* (New York: Grove Press, 1996), 15–16.

3. Ibid., 17.

4. Ibid., 46.

5. There are four published volumes of these sermons, beginning with Martin Luther King, *Strength to Love* (New York: Harper and Row, 1963).

6. Vincent Wimbush, "Introduction: Reading Darkness, Reading Scriptures," in *African Americans and the Bible: Sacred Texts and Social Textures*, ed. V. Wimbush (New York, Continuum, 2001), 15.

7. Jerma A. Jackson, *Singing in My Soul: Black Gospel Music in a Secular Age* (Chapel Hill: University of North Carolina Press, 2004), 131.

8. Barbara A. Holmes, *Joy Unspeakable: Contemplative Practices of the Black Church* (Minneapolis: Fortress Press, 2004), 91.

9. Nicole Marie Richardson, Krissah William, and Hamil R. Harris, "The Business of Faith," www.blackenterprise.com, May 2006, accessed December 2006.

10. John Blake, "Not all at seminary welcome bishop, graduation invite provokes protests." *Atlanta Journal-Constitution*, May 11, 2006, A1.

11. Scott Thumma, Dave Travis, and Warren Bird, "Megachurches Today 2005, Summary of Research Findings," http://hirr.hartsem.edu/megachurch/megastoday2005, accessed December 2006.

12. Richardson et al., "Business of Faith."

13. http://www.newbirth.org, accessed December 2006.

14. http//www.itc.edu/, accessed December 2006.

15. John Blake, "Long rebuts criticism at graduation," *Atlanta Journal-Constitution*, May 14, 2006, C1.

16. W. E. B. Du Bois, *The Souls of Black Folk* (New York: Bantam Books, 1989), 57.

17. Cornel West, *Race Matters* (Boston: Beacon Press, 1993), 14.

18. Isabel Wilkerson, "A Dollar and a Dream," *Essence* vol. 36, no. 5 (December 2005), 166–70.

CHAPTER 4

1. Jill Watts, *God, Harlem U.S.A.: The Father Divine Story* (Berkeley: University of California Press, 1992), 22.

2. Ibid., 23.

3. Darnise C. Martin, *Beyond Christianty: African Americans in a New Thought Church (Religion, Race, and Ethnicity)* (New York: New York University Press, 2005), 10–17.

4. Zora Neale Hurston, *The Sanctified Church* (Berkeley: Turtle Island, 1981), 103.

5. Matthew S. Hedstrom, "Rufus Jones and Mysticism for the Masses," *Crosscurrents* vol. 54, no. 2 (Summer 2004).

6. Gayraud Wilmore, *Black Religion and Black Radicalism: An Interpretation of the Religious History of Afro-American People* (Maryknoll, N.Y.: Orbis Books, 1993), 106.

7. Bishop Dr. S. C. ("Precious Daddy") Madison, *The Truth and Facts of the United House of Prayer for All People*, special edition, May 2006 (Pictorial revue), VII.

8. John O Hodges, "Charles Manuel 'Sweet Daddy' Grace," in *African American Religious Thought, an Anthology*, ed. Cornel West and Eddie S. Glaude Jr. (Louisville: Westminster John Knox Press, 2003), 607–08.

9. Ibid., 615.

10. Ibid., 613.

11. Religious Movements Homepage, http://religiousmovements.lib.virginia.edu/nrms/daddy_grace.html, accessed December 2006.

12. Hodges, "Charles Manuel 'Sweet Daddy' Grace," 613.

13. Jill Watts, *God, Harlem U.S.A.*, 5–6.

14. Robert Weisbrot, *Father Divine and the Struggle for Racial Equality* (Urbana: University of Illinois Press, 1983), 9–10.

15. Ibid., 16.

16. Ibid., 16–17.

17. Watts, *God, Harlem U.S.A.*, 34.

18. Ibid., 35–38.

19. Frank Byrd, "The 'Kingdom' Banquets," for the American Life Histories manuscripts, Federal Writers' Project, 1936–40, November 14, 1948, http://lcweb2.loc.gov/cgi-bin/query/D?wpa:1:./temp/~ammem_mz JW::, accessed July 2006.

20. Weisbrot, *Father Divine and the Struggle*, 122–23.

21. "Grace to Harlem," *Time*, March 7, 1938; http://www.time.com/time/magazine/article/0,9171,759210,00.html, accessed December 2006.

22. Marcus Garvey, "Africa for the Africans," reprinted in *The Norton Anthology of African American Literature*, ed. Henry Louis Gates Jr. and Nellie Y. McKay (New York: W.W. Norton, 2004, 2nd ed.), 998, emphasis mine.

23. Wilmore, *Black Religion*, 147.

24. Randall K. Burkett, "The Religious Ethos of the Universal Negro Improvement Association," in *African American Religious Studies: An Interdisciplinary Anthology*, ed. Gayraud S. Wilmore (Durham: Duke University Press 1992), 75–76.

25. Wilmore, *Black Religion*, 149–50.

26. Shelley McIntosh, *Mtoto House, Vision to Victory* (Lanham, Md.: Hamilton Books, 2005), 8.

27. Ibid., 125–26.

28. James Forman, "Manifesto to the White Christian Churches and the Jewish Synagogues in the United States of America and All Other Racist Institutions," in *Modern Black Nationalism: From Marcus Garvey to Louis Farrakhan*, ed. William Van Deburg (New York: New York University Press, 1997), 183.

29. Wilmore, *Black Religion*, 206.

30. Arnold Schucter, *Reparations: The Black Manifesto and Its Challenge to White America* (Philadelphia: J.B. Lippincott, 1970), x.

31. Jerrilyn M. McGregory, *"There Are Other Ways to Get Happy": African-American Urban Folklore*, (Ann Arbor, Mich.: UMI, 1992), 200.

CHAPTER 5

1. Kenneth E. Hagin, *Godliness is Profitable* (Tulsa: Kenneth Hagin Ministries, 1982), back matter.

2. Milmon Harrison, *Righteous Riches* (New York: Oxford University Press, 2005), 7.

3. Ibid., 8.

4. Ibid., 9.

5. Ibid., 12.

6. Kenneth Copeland, *Prosperity: The Choice Is Yours* (Fort Worth: Kenneth Copeland Publications, 1985), 11–12.

7. "Pentecostal Bedlam," http://youtube.com/watch?v=AjujnAs-6tm, accessed November 2006; "Kenneth Hagin e a 'UnÁ„o do Riso,'" ["Holy Laughter and Spiritual Drunkenness"] http://www.youtube.com/watch?v=kESE8wjEXCQ, accessed March 18, 2007.

8. Harrison, *Righteous Riches*, 10–11.

9. Leroy Thompson Sr., *Money Cometh to the Body of Christ* (Tulsa: Harrison House, 1999).

10. Ibid., 247.

11. Ibid., 250.

12. Isabel Wilkerson, "A Dollar and a Dream," *Essence* vol. 36, no. 5 (December 2005), 166–170.

13. Analysis of the sexism in black churches is the focus of other studies, notably Kelly Brown Douglas, *Sexuality and the Black Church* (Maryknoll, N.Y.: Orbis Books, 1999).

14. Taffi L. Dollar, "Far Above Rubies: The Price of a Virtuous Woman" in *Changing Your World* vol. 3, no. 5 (May 2001), 19.

15. Ibid.

16. Ibid., 15. This is a reference to C. Dollar's Covenant Connection argument.

17. Ibid., 20.

18. Ibid., 19.

19. Creflo A. Dollar Jr., *The Covenant Connector: How to Get Connected to the Promises of God through the Tithe* (College Park, Ga.: Creflo Dollar Publications, 1997), 33.

20. Ed Donnally, "He's Still Not Afraid to Confront," *Charisma Magazine* (August, 2000); http://www.charismamag.com/display.php?id=456&print=yes.

21. Frederick K. C. Price, *Race, Religion, and Racism: A Bold Encounter with Division in the Church* (Los Angeles: Dr. Frederick K. C. Price Ministries, 1999), 4–5.

CHAPTER 6

1. From "Unity History," www.unityonline.org/discover_history.htm.
2. "5 Basic Unity Principles," www.unity.org/5principles.html.
3. Johnnie Colemon, *It Works If You Work It*, front matter in five work books, transcribed by Rosalie Jackson (Chicago: Christ Universal Temple, no date), iii.
4. Darnise C. Martin, *Beyond Christianity: African Americans in a New Thought Church* (New York: New York University Press, 2005), 151.
5. Colemon, *It Works If You Work It*, iv.
6. Ibid., back matter.
7. It was not clear in my research whether or not this seminary is accredited.
8. Colemon, *It Works If You Work It*, volume 1, v.
9. Ibid., 1.
10. Ibid., 3.
11. Ibid., 9.
12. Ibid., 15.
13. Ibid., volume 2, 8.
14. Milmon Harrison, *Righteous Riches* (New York: Oxford University Press, 2005), 135, emphasis mine.
15. Martin, *African Americans in a New Thought Church*, 152.
16. Barbara King, www.drbarbara.info/.
17. Ibid.
18. Marion Delaney-Harris, "About the Author," in Barbara King, *Transform Your Life* (New York: Perigree Books, 1995), 189–90.
19. Barbara King, *Transform Your Life* (New York: Perigree Books, 1995), 80.
20. Ibid., 83.
21. Ibid.
22. Ibid., 88–89.
23. Ibid., 127–28.
24. Ibid., 92, 103.
25. James Reid, "Dr. Ernest Holmes: The First Religious Scientist," www.religiousscience.org/ucrs_site/our_founder/first_religious.html, accessed January 2007.
26. Martin, *African Americans in a New Thought Church*, 110, 113–14.
27. Martin, *African Americans in a New Thought Church*, 109.
28. Frederick Eikerenkoetter, *Health, Joy, and Prosperity for You* (New York: self published, no date), 88, 89–90.

29. J. H. Sammis (lyrics), and D. B. Towner (music), "Trust and Obey," 1887.

30. *Rev. Ike's Miracles Right Now!* #020103 (Boston: United Christian Evangelistic Association, 1999), 12.

31. *Science of Living Study Guide*, vol 3, no. 2 (December 1972, January/February 1973), 13–14.

32. Eikerenkoetter, *Health, Joy, and Prosperity for You*, 35.

33. Ibid., 36–37.

34. Rev. Ike, *The Miracle Money Book Shows You How to Plant Money Seeds*, 4th ed., #100100 (Boston, no date), 3.

35. Ibid., 27.

36. "Declaration of Our Awakened World," under the topic "Source Document," http://www.agnt.org, accessed December 2006.

37. Martin, 143–44.

CHAPTER 7

1. W. E. B. Du Bois, *The Souls of Black Folk* (New York: Bantam Books, 1989, first published in 1903), 57.

2. Michael Eric Dyson, *Race Rules* (Reading, Mass.: Addison-Wesley, 1996), 189.

3. Lee H. Butler Jr. "The Unpopular Experience of Popular Culture: Cultural Resistance as Identity Formation," *Journal of Pastoral Theology* vol. 11, no. 1 (June 2001), 48–49.

4. Garth Kasimu Baker-Fletcher, *Xodus: An African American Male Journey* (Minneapolis: Fortress Press, 1996), 160.

5. Stanley Aronowitz, *How Class Works* (New Haven: Yale University Press, 2003), 22.

6. Milmon Harrison, *Righteous Riches* (New York: Oxford University Press, 2005), 148–49.

7. bell hooks, *Killing Rage: Ending Racism* (New York: Henry Holt and Company, 1995), 29.

8. Taffi L. Dollar, "Far Above Rubies: The Price of a Virtuous Woman" in *Changing Your World* vol. 3, no. 5 (May 2001), 20.

9. Kelly Brown Douglas, *Sexuality and the Black Church, A Womanist Perspective* (Maryknoll, N.Y.: Orbis Books, 1999), 80–81.

10. Toinette M. Eugene, "In This Here Place, We Flesh: Womanist Ruminations on Embodied Experience and Expressions," *Daughters of Sarah* vol. 22, no. 1 (Winter 1996), 14–15.

11. Iva Carruthers, "The Black Church in the Age of False Prophets: An Interview with Gayraud Wilmore" in *Blow the Trumpet in Zion: Global Vision and Action for the 21st-Century Black Church*, ed. Iva E. Carruthers, Frederick D. Haynes III, and Jeremiah A Wright Jr. (Minneapolis: Fortress Press, 2005), 170–71.

CHAPTER 8

1. Creflo Dollar, *The Covenant Connector: How to Get Connected to the Promises of God through the Tithe* (College Park, Ga.: Creflo Dollar Publications, 1997), 74.

2. Ibid., 62.

3. Joshua Levs, "America's Black Churches Debate Role in Society," August 17, 2005, http://www.voanews.com/english/archive/2005-08/2005-08-17-voa22.cfm?renderforprint, accessed January 2007.

4. Kelly Brown Douglas, *What's Faith Got to Do With It? Black Bodies/Christian Souls* (Maryknoll, N.Y.: Orbis Books, 2005), 28.

5. Ibid., 200, 202.

6. Dwight N. Hopkins, *Being Human: Race, Culture, and Religion* (Minneapolis: Fortress Press, 2005), 167.

7. Ibid., 166.

8. Emilie M. Townes, *Womanist Ethics and the Cultural Production of Evil* (New York: Palgrave Macmillan, 2006), 159.

9. Delores S. Williams, "Straight Talk, Plain Talk: Womanist Words about Salvation in a Social Context," in *Embracing the Spirit: Womanist Perspectives on Hope, Salvation, and Transformation* ed. E. Townes (Maryknoll, N,Y.: Orbis Books, 1997), 98.

10. Ibid.

11. Ibid., 99–100.

12. Obery M. Hendricks Jr., "The Prophetic Imperative: Reclaiming the Gospel by Speaking Truth to Power" in Carruthers et al, *Blow the Trumpet in Zion*, 82–84.

13 Otis Moss III, "Discerning among Theologies in the Black Church," in Carruthers et al, *Blow the Trumpet in Zion*, 156–58.

BIBLIOGRAPHY

Andrews, Marcellus. *The Political Economy of Hope and Fear: Capitalism and the Black Condition in America.* New York: New York University Press, 1999.

Aronowitz, Stanley. *How Class Works.* New Haven: Yale University Press, 2003.

Baker-Fletcher, Garth Kasimu. *Xodus: An African American Male Journey.* Minneapolis: Fortress Press, 1996.

Blake, John. "Long rebuts criticism at graduation." *Atlanta Journal-Constitution.* May 14, 2006, C1.

_____. "Not all at seminary welcome bishop, graduation invite provokes protests." *Atlanta Journal-Constitution.* May 11, 2006, A1.

Bridges, Flora. *Resurrection Song: African-American Spirituality.* Maryknoll, N.Y.: Orbis Books, 2001.

Burkett, Randall K. "The Religious Ethos of the Universal Negro Improvement Association." In *African American Religious Studies: An Interdisciplinary Anthology.* Ed. Gayraud S. Wilmore. Durham: Duke University Press 1992, 60–81.

Butler, Lee H., Jr. "The Unpopular Experience of Popular Culture: Cultural Resistance as Identity Formation." *Journal of Pastoral Theology.* vol. 11, no. 1 (June 2001), 40–44.

Byrd, Frank. "American Life Histories" manuscripts. Federal Writers' Project, 1936–40. November 14, 1948, http://lcweb2.loc.gov/cgi-bin/query/D?wpa:1:./temp/~ammem_mzJW:: Accessed July 2006.

Carruthers, Iva E., Frederick D. Haynes III, and Jeremiah A Wright Jr., eds. *Blow the Trumpet in Zion: Global Vision and Action for the 21st-Century Black Church.* Minneapolis: Fortress Press, 2005.

Colemon, Johnnie. *It Works If You Work It.* Five work books, transcribed by Rosalie Jackson. Chicago: Christ Universal Temple, no date.

Cone, James H. *God of the Oppressed.* New York: Seabury Press, 1975.

Copeland, Kenneth. *Prosperity: The Choice Is Yours.* Fort Worth: Kenneth Copeland Publications, 1985.

Coquet, Cècile. "My God Is a Time-God: How African American Folk Oratory Speaks (of) Time." In *African Americans and the Bible: Sacred Texts and Social Textures*. Ed. Vincent Wimbush. New York: Continuum, 2001. 514–35.

di Leonardo, Micaela. "White Lies, Black Myths: Rape, Race, and the Black 'Underclass.'" In *The Gender Sexuality Reader*. Ed. Roger N. Lancaster and Micaela di Leonardo. New York: Routledge, 1997. 53–68.

Dollar, Creflo A. Jr. *The Covenant Connector: How to Get Connected to the Promises of God through the Tithe*. College Park, Ga.: Creflo Dollar Publications, 1997.

_____. *The Divine Order of Faith: How to Get from the Problem to the Answer*. College Park, Ga.: Creflo Dollar Publications, 1993.

Dollar, Taffi L. "Far Above Rubies: The Price of a Virtuous Woman." In *Changing Your World*. vol. 3, no. 5. (May 2001).

Douglas, Kelly Brown. *Sexuality and the Black Church: A Womanist Perspective*. Maryknoll, N.Y.: Orbis Books, 1999.

_____. *What's Faith Got to Do with It? Black Bodies/Christian Souls*. Maryknoll, N.Y.: Orbis Books, 2005.

Du Bois, W. E. B. *The Souls of Black Folk*. New York: Bantam Books, 1989.

Dyson, Michael Eric. *I May Not Get There with You: The True Martin Luther King Jr*. New York: Free Press, 2000.

_____. *Race Rules*. Reading, Mass.: Addison-Wesley Publishing Co., 1996.

Eikerenkoetter, Frederick. *Health, Joy, and Prosperity for You*. New York: self-published, no date.

Eugene, Toinette M. "In This Here Place, We Flesh: Womanist Ruminations on Embodied Experience and Expressions," *Daughters of Sarah*, vol. 22, no. 1 (Winter 1996), 14–15.

Forman, James. "Manifesto to the White Christian Churches and the Jewish Synagogues in the United States of America and All Other Racist Institutions." In *Modern Black Nationalism: from Marcus Garvey to Louis Farrakhan*. Ed. William Van Deburg. New York: New York University Press, 1997, 182–8-7.

Frazier, E. Franklin. *The Negro Church in America*. New York: Schocken Books, 1974.

Garvey, Marcus. "Africa for the Africans." In *The Norton Anthology of African American Literature*. Ed. Henry Louis Gates Jr. and Nellie Y. McKay. New York: W.W. Norton, 2004, 2nd ed., 998.

"Grace to Harlem," March 7, 1938. Http://www.time.com/time/magazine/article/0,9171,759210,00.html. Accessed December 2006.

Graves, Earl. *How to Succeed in Business without Being White: Straight Talk on Making It in America.* New York: Harper, 1997.

Hagin, Kenneth E. *Godliness Is Profitable.* Tulsa: Kenneth Hagin Ministries, 1982.

Harrison, Milmon F. *Righteous Riches: The Word of Faith Movement in Contemporary African American Religion.* New York: Oxford University Press, 2005.

Hedstrom, Matthew S. "Rufus Jones and Mysticism for the Masses." *Crosscurrents* vol. 54, no. 2 (Summer 2004).

Higginbotham, Evelyn Brooks. *Righteous Discontent: The Women's Movement in the Black Baptist Church 1880–1920.* Cambridge: Harvard University Press, 1993.

Hodges, John O. "Charles Manuel 'Sweet Daddy' Grace." In *African American Religious Thought: An Anthology.* Ed. Cornel West and Eddie S. Glaude Jr. Louisville: Westminster John Knox Press, 2003, 605–15.

Holmes, Barbara A. *Joy Unspeakable: Contemplative Practices of the Black Church.* Minneapolis: Fortress Press, 2004.

hooks, bell. *Killing Rage: Ending Racism.* New York: Henry Holt and Company, 1995.

Hopkins, Dwight N. *Being Human: Race, Culture, and Religion.* Minneapolis: Augsburg Fortress Press, 2005.

Hurston, Zora Neale. *The Sanctified Church.* Berkeley: Turtle Island, 1981.

Ike, Rev. *The Miracle Money Book Shows You How to Plant Money Seeds.* 4th ed. # 100100. Boston, no date.

_____. *Rev. Ike's Miracles Right Now!* #020103. Boston: United Christian Evangelistic Association, 1999.

Jackson, Jerma A. *Singing in My Soul: Black Gospel Music in a Secular Age.* Chapel Hill: University of North Carolina Press, 2004.

Jacobs, Claude F. "Rituals of Healing in African American Spiritual Churches." In *Religion and Healing in America.* Ed. Linda L. Barnes and Susan S. Sered. New York: Oxford University Press, 2005. 333–42.

Kimbro, Dennis, and Napoleon Hill. *Think and Grow Rich: A Black Choice.* New York: Ballantine Books, 1997.

King, Barbara. *Transform Your Life.* New York: Perigree Books, 1995.

King-Hammond, Leslie. "The Bible and the Aesthetics of Sacred Space in Twentieth-Century African American Experience." In *African Americans and the Bible: Sacred Texts and Social Textures.* Ed. Vincent L. Wimbush. New York: Continuum, 2001. 433–47.

Lawrence, Beverly Hall. *Reviving the Spirit: A Generation of African Americans Goes Home to Church.* New York: Grove Press, 1996.

Levs, Joshua. "America's Black Churches Debate Role in Society." August 17, 2005, http://www.voanews.com/english/archive/2005-08/2005-08-17-voa22.cfm?renderforprint. Accessed January 2007.

Lewis, Reginald, and Blair S. Walker. *"Why Should White Guys Have All the Fun?":: How Reginald Lewis Created a Billion Dollar Business Empire.* New York: John Wiley and Sons, 1995.

Lincoln, C. Eric. *The Black Church Since Frazier.* New York: Schocken Books, 1974.

Madison, Bishop Dr. S. C. ("Precious Daddy"). *The Truth and Facts of the United House of Prayer for All People.* Pictorial revue, special ed., May 2006.

Marable, Manning. *Living Black History: How Reimagining the African-American Past Can Remake America's Racial Future.* New York: Basic Civitas Books, 2006.

Martin, Darnise C. *Beyond Christianty: African Americans in a New Thought Church.* New York: New York University Press, 2005.

Martin, Joan M. *More Than Chains or Toil: A Christian Work Ethic of Enslaved Women.* Louisville: Westminster John Knox Press, 2000.

McGregory, Jerrilyn M. *"There Are Other Ways to Get Happy:" African-American Urban Folklore.* Ann Arbor, Mich.: UMI, 1992.

McIntosh, Shelley. *Mtoto House, Vision to Victory.* Lanham, Md.: Hamilton Books 2005.

National Urban League. *The State of Black America 2005: Prescriptions for Change.* Ed. Lee Daniels. Available at http://www.nul.org/thestateof blackamerica.html.

"Pentecostal Bedlam." http://youtube.com/watch?v=AjujnAs-6tm. Accessed November 2006. "Kenneth Hagin e a 'UnÁ„o do Riso,'" ["Holy Laughter and Spiritual Drunkenness"] http://www.youtube.com/watch?v=kESE 8wjEXCQ. Accessed March 18, 2007.

Price, Frederick K. C. *Race, Religion, and Racism: A Bold Encounter with Division in the Church.* Los Angeles: Dr. Frederick K. C. Price Ministries, 1999.

Religious Movements Homepage, http://religiousmovements.lib.virginia .edu/nrms/daddy_grace.html. Accessed December 2006

Richardson, Nicole Marie, Krissah William, and Hamil R. Harris. "The Business of Faith." www.blackenterprise.com, May 2006. Accessed December 2006.

Riley, Ann L. "Health and Self-Esteem among African Americans." *African American Research Perspectives* vol. 9, no. 1 (Winter 2003), 158.

Schucter, Arnold. *Reparations: The Black Manifesto and Its Challenge to White America.* Philadelphia: J.B. Lippincott, 1970.

Smiley, Tavis, ed. *The Covenant with Black America.* Chicago: Third World Press 2006.

Steinberg, Stephen. "The Liberal Retreat from Race during the Post–Civil Rights Era." In *The House That Race Built: Black Americans, U.S. Terrain.* Ed. Wahneema Lubiano. New York: Pantheon Books, 1997, 13–47.

Thompson, Leroy Sr. *Money Cometh to the Body of Christ*. Tulsa: Harrison House 1999.

Thumma, Scott, Dave Travis, and Warren Bird. "Megachurches Today 2005, Summary of Research Findings." http://hirr.hartsem.edu/mega church/megastoday2005. Accessed December 2006.

Townes, Emilie M. *Womanist Ethics and the Cultural Production of Evil*. New York: Palgrave Macmillan, 2006.

Walker, Alice. "Introduction: Sweet Honey in the Rock—The Sound of Our Own Culture." In Bernice Johnson Reagon and Sweet Honey in the Rock. *We Who Believe in Freedom: Sweet Honey in the Rock Still on the Journey*. New York: Anchor Books, 1993). 7–10.

Watts, Jill. *God, Harlem U.S.A.: The Father Divine Story*. Berkeley: University of California Press, 1992.

Weems, Robert J. Jr. *Desegregating the Dollar: African American Consumerism in the Twentieth Century*. New York: New York University Press 1998.

Weisbrot, Robert. *Father Divine and the Struggle for Racial Equality*. Urbana: University of Illinois Press, 1983.

West, Cornel. "Nihilism in Black America." In *Black Popular Culture*. Ed. Gina Dent. Seattle: Bay Press, 1992. 37–47.

_____. *Race Matters*. Boston: Beacon Press, 1993.

Wilkerson, Isabel. "A Dollar and a Dream." *Essence* vol. 36, no. 5 (December 2005), 166–70.

Williams, Delores S. "Straight Talk, Plain Talk: Womanist Words about Salvation in a Social Context." In *Embracing the Spirit: Womanist Perspectives on Hope, Salvation, and Transformation*. Ed. E. Townes. Maryknoll: Orbis Books, 1997. 97–121.

Wilmore, Gayraud. *Black Religion and Black Radicalism: An Interpretation of the Religious History of Afro-American People*. Maryknoll, N.Y.: Orbis Books, 1993.

Wimbush, Vincent, ed. *African Americans and the Bible: Sacred Texts and Social Textures*. New York, Continuum 2001.

Woodson, Carter G. *The History of the Negro Church*. Washington, D.C.: Associated Publishers, 1921.